CHINESE RESTAURANT
COOKBOOK

CHINESE RESTAURANT COOKBOOK

PAT CHAPMAN

PIATKUS

ACKNOWLEDGEMENTS

The publishers would like to thank the following for the loan of props for the photographs:

David Reel of Grayshott Pottery, Grayshott, Hindhead, Surrey
Neal Street East, Covent Garden, London WC2
Christina and Mr Kahn of the New World Chinese Restaurant, 1 Gerrards Place, London W1
Cheryl Benford

First published in 1990 by
Judy Piatkus (Publishers) Ltd
5 Windmill Street, London W1P 1HF

First paperback edition 1991

British Library Cataloguing in Publication Data
Chapman, Pat *1940–*
The Curry Club chinese restaurant cookbook.
1. Food. Chinese dishes. Recipes
I. Title
641.5951

ISBN 0–7499–1016–X
ISBN 0–7499–1102–6 (Pbk)

Edited by Heather Rocklin
Designed by Paul Saunders
Illustrated by Hanife Hassan-O'Keeffe and Paul Saunders
Photography by Tim Imrie
Word processing and photographic concepts by
Dominique Davis

Phototypeset in $10\frac{1}{2}/12\frac{1}{2}$ Monophoto Photina
Printed and bound in Great Britain by
Butler & Tanner Ltd, Frome, Somerset

CONTENTS

INTRODUCTION

Although I have been going to Indian restaurants since I was a child, in the late 1940s, I must confess that my first visit to a Chinese restaurant did not take place until the 1960s. I mention this because I can still vividly remember the occasion to this day. I was very familiar with the Indian menu, but the Chinese menu was to me at that time more than a little bewildering and confusing.

Because one always plumps for what one knows, I ordered a curry. Of course it was totally different to the Indian restaurant curry which I knew and loved, and I felt a great sense of disappointment. Chinese food was not for me, I thought. Fortunately, not long after my first venture as described, I started travelling around the world on business and I found myself in Singapore and Hong Kong with some great friends of mine who knew about Chinese food. They decided to educate me.

We not only visited the best restaurants but we also toured the fabulous and equally famous open-air food stalls where we watched the food being prepared in front of us. I marvelled at the freshness of the raw ingredients and the dexterity of the cooks who tossed the contents of their woks high into the air then deftly caught them whilst at the same time flambeing them in a spectacular whoosh of fire. For such spontaneity, however, considerable preparation had to take place. Watching that was exciting too. But it was the final cooking that impressed me most; in seconds it was done and what a spectacle it was. I was converted!

Indeed, it was those spectacular scenes which triggered me to start collecting recipes. There and then I decided to write down the ingredients and method of any item of food which took my fancy. In a very short space of time I had hundreds of scraps of paper with scribbles all over them. They contained recipes from many different countries and culinary styles.

During the 1960s it was not easy to find either Chinese or Indian restaurants in any but the largest cities. During the 1970s all this changed. They were to be found everywhere. I made a point of trying a new one whenever I visited a particular place and right from the start I asked to visit the kitchens. In the early days this usually met with a polite refusal, but fortunately not from everyone. I discovered that people whose business is food generally enjoy talking about food and demonstrating it, and despite the obvious language barriers I found myself learning an incredible amount of useful things simply by talking to chefs and restaurateurs.

It probably does not come as a surprise to anyone that most of the recipes and tips I collected initially were curry oriented. But by the end of the 1970s I was astonished to find that I had amassed a substantial collection of Chinese recipes too.

The idea to produce a recipe book on Chinese food has been with me for a long time. It was the food at the good Chinese restaurants that I enjoyed and that I wanted to re-create at home but no books had been written on the subject. Indeed at that stage there were precious few cookbooks about Chinese food at all. Now there are plenty, all dealing with various aspects of authentic Chinese cooking. But, as far as I know, this is the first cookbook to give the secrets of the Chinese restaurants.

To select the 150 or so most popular recipes from my collection, I have examined the menus from about 200 good Chinese restaurants, not only in the UK but in the USA, Australia and Europe as well. I have also discussed the concept with Chinese restaurateurs and chefs and have asked them what their most popular dishes are. I have endeavoured to include them all in this book. In addition I have included a fascinating selection of special dishes.

I hope you'll find this book breaks through the 'inscrutability barrier' to provide you with the inside knowledge necessary to recreate at home any-thing from a prawn cracker to a full multi-course banquet without having to resort to the local takeaway and at a fraction of the cost. The dishes are fun to make and serve and you will gain great satisfaction from the achievement.

I hope you will not be able to resist chopsticking your way through all its pages.

Pat Chapman
Founder
The Curry Club
April 1990

CHAPTER 1

CULINARY BACKGROUND

China is the world's most highly populated country. It is also the birthplace of one of the world's earliest civilisations and of paper-making, gunpowder, fireworks, the compass, Confucius, the wok and the giant panda.

China's land mass is larger than Europe and the USA combined, and its population of 1 billion is nearly double. Yet all Chinese speak the same language (albeit in a variety of dialects), use the same script, share the same culture, the same physical appearance and, by and large, the same culinary background.

This quite remarkable preservation of identity is virtually unique amongst the populations of the Old World and is largely due to the country's relative isolation.

China's isolation was the result of geography rather than design. Her people occupied a huge fertile portion of land that was divided from other groups of people by the Himalayas to the south (Indo-China was largely unpopulated then) and, in central Asia, thousands of miles of inhospitable deserts, mountains, forests and steppes.

As thousands of years went by even these inhospitable zones became occupied by uncivilised violent warring tribes. The Mongols in the North were one such people who were so much of a threat that by the third century BC the emperor of the day ordered that an extensive wall be built. It was over 2,400 km (1,500 miles) in length. Much of the Great Wall, which was built at the cost of thousands of slave lives, still remains to this day, having been substantially rebuilt in the fifteenth century.

The nearest civilizations of the day, those in India and the Middle East, Egypt and Mesopotamia, were so inaccessible as to be virtually non-existent to each other. Occasionally adventurous travellers and small incursive war parties got through, with their tales of the ways of the West. By 500 BC an emperor of the Zhou dynasty came to learn of the wonder that was the horse. Until then China had neither seen nor heard of such a beast. The emperor badly wanted to equip his armies with the horse. The problem was how to obtain these magnificent creatures. The emperor decreed that they should be procured by trading not war. The problem was that the nearest trading kingdoms were in the Mediterranean, some 9,654 km (6,000) miles from China's then capital of Xian on the eastern seaboard.

It was necessary to establish a route with many fortified stopping places complete with troops and a water supply. Thousands of these were eventually established. In the event there was a main route with several diversions which traversed deserts, mountains, forests and steppes and linked ancient major cities all along the way. China's principal exports were beautifully crafted artifacts in jade, bronze and lacquered wood, and furs, dried fruit, nuts and valuable spices such as cassia bark. By far the most prolific export was Chinese silk and it was not surprising therefore that the route became known as the Silk Route or Road.

The Chinese obtained their horses, along with gold, silver, ivory, jewels, coral, glass, walnuts, almonds, broad beans, onions, cucumbers and grapes and spices such as pepper and cummin.

By 100 BC the Silk Route was at its height supplying the Roman Empire. It was incredibly busy with endless loads of goods travelling in both directions. It took over two years for the goods to traverse the route from one end to the other, although few people would actually do the journey from end to end and back again. The Chinese merchant in Xian city would sell his merchandise to middlemen, and so on up and down the line. The network was populated with a chain of merchants, agents and middlemen, culminating at the western end with Arab traders.

China escaped the humiliation of colonial conquest by the Europeans, but its Silk Route, which lasted for two thousand years, faded into oblivion at around the time that China's greatest dynasty, the Ming dynasty (1368–1644) was in disintegration and China receded back into isolation.

The crisis of poverty and over-population eventually caused a relatively substantial outflow of Chinese who went to work for the new colonialists. In the nineteenth century Chinese travelled to all corners of the world: they went to Malaya to work in the tin mines, to Australia to work in the gold mines, and to the USA to build the railways. They also became established as sailors on the rapidly expanding merchant navy networks. Most of these emigrants and seamen came from Southern China, specifically the provinces of Guangdong and Fujian.

Today it is estimated that around 60 million Chinese live outside China. As a percentage of China's population this is a mere unnoticable 0.6%, yet 60 million is more than the population of Great Britain. Little wonder then that Chinese restaurants abroad are so prevalent and Chinese food so well known all over the world.

CULINARY ACHIEVEMENT

China has a history of continuous culinary development. Archaeologists have found the site of the capital city of the first Chinese dynasty, Xian, dating back to 2100 BC. The remains of cooked chicken and carp were found as well as cooked elephant bones!

During the Zhou dynasty (1122–255 BC) Chinese agriculturalists learned to cultivate rice, wheat, melons, squashes and celery. It was also during this era that soya beans were farmed and processed into all manner of products including sauces and pastes (see pages 35 and 39–40). Sheep and boar were farmed and roasted. During the Han dynasty (206 BC–220 AD), noodles and bean curd were invented.

The frying of rice and noodles and dim sum steaming techniques and with it the stackable dim sum steamer basket were invented during the Sui dynasty (518–618 AD).

The wok had been invented centuries before Christ but it was considerably refined during the Tang dynasty (618–907 AD) when stir-frying was perfected. Also during this period the Chinese learned to distil spirits.

During the Song dynasty (960–1279 AD) Chinese vinegars and rice wines were developed and rice growing commenced in the South.

China's most opulent and magnificent dynasty, the Mings, ruled in Peking from 1368–1644 and modern Chinese cooking was developed during this era. To this day Pekinese cuisine is regarded as the *haute cuisine* of China, and this came about because of the demands of the respective Ming emperors.

Upon the overthrow of the Mings in 1644, China's final dynasty, the Quing dynasty (1644–1911), was established in Canton. At first little culinary development took place. Later a light, fast and sophisticated cooking style evolved and today's Cantonese cuisine emerged.

Four thousand years of imperial rule came abruptly to an end in 1911 with the establishment of the People's Republic of China. Following the 1949 revolution this became the Chinese People's Republic. For over 30 years, *haute cuisine* and restaurants were regarded as elitist, reactionary and Imperialist. The supply of certain ingredients was forbidden. Sesame, nuts, pulses and some grains were in this category. Meat and poultry became virtually unobtainable. A great many restaurants were forced to close. The population of China came near to starvation. China's food production has always been on the knife-edge of success. Only 7% of the nation's land mass is suitable for farming and most of that is given over to vegetable cultivation. Rice, sweet potato and the ubiquitous soya bean are the most prolific crops. So the regime's tampering simply made matters worse.

It was not until 1982, a few years after the death of Mao Tse-tung (Communist Party chairman), that things began to improve. Forbidden fruits and foodstuffs began to reappear and restaurants and tea houses started to open. The going was not that easy, however, as there was a shortage of skilled labour, farmers and cooks. A generation had passed since the restrictions had been imposed and vital knowledge was lost. Recently the Chinese government has implemented training schemes and encouraged regrowth.

It is significant that during this exact period of stagnation in China itself, 1949–1982, the Chinese restaurant abroad expanded so significantly. In Hong Kong for example there are now over 40,000 restaurants, many of them Chinese. This reflects a tenfold expansion in 30 years. In Britain the number of Chinese restaurants grew from a handful to 7,000 in the same space of time, and a similar thing has been happening elsewhere in nearly every free country in the world.

Chinese philosophy and food

In essence, the Chinese seek perfection in all aspects of life. In this respect everything to do with the intellect and the body is valued equally and without distinction. This includes philosophy, mysticism, religion, scientific learning, and arts and crafts. It also includes the fitness of the body, nutrition, diet and cooking.

At the beginning of their civilisation the ancient Chinese were totally convinced that their land was at the centre of the universe. The unification of China and the establishment of the Imperial dynasties from around 2100 BC did nothing to change this philosophy and thus the emperors were held to be god-like and all powerful.

Somewhat later, Taoism came into being and it teaches that the universe came into existence at around 600 BC. This somewhat confusingly places it in the middle of the Zhou dynasty (1122–255 BC). The precepts of Taoism were written in the fourth century BC in the learned work the I Ching (Book of Changes). It states that everything is in a state of balance of negative and positive concepts – Yin and Yang.

Interestingly Buddhism was founded in India at around the same time as Taoism was founded in China. It reached China by the first century AD and reinforced the principals of Yin and Yang.

The concept of Yin and Yang is one of harmonious contrast and balance. This harmony is defined as falling into three groups: those of Yin, those of Yang and those of the combined Yin-yang.

Yin is cooling, Yang is heating and Yin-yang is neutral. In human terms a Yin person is quiet and introverted, and a calming influence. A Yang person is active, extroverted, creative and excitable. A Yin-yang person is pragmatic, careful in decision and liable to stay on the fence.

In the culinary art, every ingredient falls into one of these three categories, the logic of which must remain with the Chinese who invented it. Yin (cooling) foods, for example, include sea salt, sugar, beer, crab, duck, spring onion and soda water. Yang (heating) foods, include ginger, chilli, smoked fish, coffee, beef and brandy, whilst Yin-yang (neutral) foods include some obvious examples like steamed rice and noodles and less obvious examples like peaches, carrots and pigeon.

Every meal should carry a perfect balance of Yin and Yang. Fortunately, selection is largely a matter of common sense. However there are some other Yin-yang principles which are worth observing. For example all ingredients must be very fresh and very clean.

There are four Yin-yang tastes: sweet, sour, bitter and salty. These tastes must always be present in a meal. In some regions a fifth taste, pungency, can be added.

There are further rules regarding the composition of a meal. The concept of *Fan-cai* states that a meal is in two parts, *fan* and *cai*. *Fan* dishes are staples including grain, rice, noodles, steamed buns and dumplings. *Cai* dishes comprise all others. The objective is to serve every meal with a balance of aroma, appearance, colour, texture and flavour.

There are no rules as to the order of dishes and there are no set courses. A typical everyday meal at home for two or four people would consist of one *fan* dish and three or four *cia* dishes with a soup. Each dish should be varied, yet complementary. For example one dish may be spicy, another mild, one may be chewy and another crisp. In general terms this might be a rich dish served with a bland one, a wet one with a dry one, a sweet taste with a savoury taste, and a smooth texture with a crisp one. The more people there are at the meal, the greater the choice of dishes that the host can offer. A good rule of thumb is to supply one dish per guest plus rice and/or noodles. The size of each dish should be the same for a group of four as for a group of eight or twelve. So the larger the group the greater the choice, with each person having a small portion of many items. This, of course, makes Chinese food absolutely perfect for the social occasion, whether it is a large group going out to a restaurant, or a special dinner party at home.

The Chinese banquet

The Mandarin emperors are on record for holding astounding banquets where 100 or more dishes were served. It was the custom to serve the dishes one at a time or in small groups, so the event must have lasted for hours and hours. It was meticulously planned so that it represented a series of culinary climaxes. A soup might be followed by a bland, soft stir-fry; subsequent dishes would lift the diners' expectations until a climactic 'big dish' such as Peking Duck would top that section of the meal. Then a soup would follow, and the whole procedure would be repeated this time with different dishes until the arrival of the next 'big dish'. Quite where the courtiers put all this food is not on record, but we can follow the same concept (as do the contemporary Chinese) on a small scale by designing our dinner party menu so that it climaxes with a 'big dish' then subsides into a relaxing conclusion. I have given some menu examples on pages 25–8.

REGIONAL COOKERY STYLES

Although the cooking of China has a uniform style, established thousands of years ago and perfected over all that time, there are regional differences. Those of us outside China have until very recently only been familiar with the cooking style of South China, centred on Canton (Guangzhou) and neighbouring Hong Kong. This is because most Chinese who travelled abroad and established their restaurants and infrastructure overseas orig inally came from the South.

The South

This region occupies the quadrant from due south to due east on the Chinese map. It has a sub-tropical climate and thousands of miles of China Sea coastline. Its main province is Guangdong (or Kwantung), of which Canton is the capital.

Cantonese cooking is not highly seasoned. Garlic and spices are avoided. Steam and water are the main cooking methods. When oil is used it is often peanut oil. The Cantonese have a very sweet tooth and sweetness is a major flavouring agent in their food. This is contrasted with sour tastes, leading to the creation of wonderful sweet and sour dishes, and savoury tastes achieved by the use of soy. It was in this region that cultivation and processing of the soya bean was developed and perfected. Hoisin sauce is the classic combination of these tastes with its mixture of rice vinegar, sugar and soya bean paste.

Main foods of the region are millet, wheat, rice, sugar, vegetables and fruit including pineapple, banana, lychees and citrus fruit. Pigs, ducks and chickens are plentiful, but are none-the-less regarded as luxuries. Fish and seafood are abundantly available, from both the coast and the widespread river network. Oyster sauce is an invention of Southern China.

The food of the region received a boost when the Imperial chefs fled to Canton with the overthrow of the Ming dynasty in 1644. Whilst the overall style remained unchanged, certain more sophisticated techniques appeared, such as the marination of food in rice wine or sweet sauces, and a greater attention to the combinations of colour, texture, aroma and flavour. Dim sum, small delicate attractive morsels such as wontons, are from this region.

Along the coast of this region and in the neighbouring island of Taiwan is a distinctly different cooking style. Called *chiu-zhou*, the food is marinated in the fermented rice grain left over from wine making. It is simmered in strong tasty stocks and served with a rice gruel. As far as I know *chiu-zhou* food is never served in the restaurants of the West. But the area does have one thing of outstanding international repute, its soy sauce. This industry is centred on the principal city, Amoy.

The East

With Shanghai its capital, this region is dominated by its very long coastline and the world's third longest river, the Yangtze. Consequently fish and shellfish are equally popular inland and near the sea. Pork and chicken are bred in this region, but vegetarian cuisine is prevalent, and vegetables always accompany meat dishes.

The presentation of food is important here and the Eastern region specialises in animal and flower carvings made from vegetables. Seasonings are light. The area was once the centre of the Imperial salt trade and salty dishes, such as Salt-baked Chicken (page 130), are greatly enjoyed. Sugar is also used in cooking, resulting in the sweetest dishes in the Chinese repertoire.

This region has the distinction that classical Chinese cooking originated here over several thousand years, and the Imperial court was based here until the fourteenth century.

Flavourings involving soy were developed here and to this day the best soy sauce comes from this region. Slow cooking in dark soy sauce (also called red cooking) is an important cooking method. The most commonly used cooking oil is peanut.

China's best black vinegar (Zhenjiang vinegar) comes from the East, as does the best rice wine (Shaoxing rice wine). This makes its appearance in many dishes including the wonderfully named Drunken Chicken (see page 128). This wine is very sour and distinctive, and it is used along with the equally distinctive rice vinegar to create the sweet and sour tastes so popular in the East.

Noodles, including special broad and long sweet noodles, and rice are the staples. Oranges and tea grow prolifically and a particular local speciality is Zhejian ham, which is rather like smoked bacon.

The North

This region is framed by mountains to the north and west. Much of the Great Wall forms the northern border. The vast Yellow River cuts through the centre of the region, and there is a substantial coastline, The principal city is Beijing (Peking).

Winters are very severe in the North, with temperatures reaching well below freezing. Spring and autumn almost invariably bring with them tempestuous storms whilst summers are generally hot. This wide variation in climate has a bearing on the food of the region. Nothing grows prolifically and the season is short. Consequently techniques have evolved for pickling and drying summer produce. Vegetables are compressed with salt and spices in large earthenware vats. Meat and fungi are dried.

The staples are grains such as wheat, corn and millet. Breadbuns, dumplings, pancakes and noodles are steam cooked. Meat is in such short supply that it is regarded as a luxury, although beef, pork and mutton are reared. Vegetables include hardy root items such as turnips and sweet potatoes, as well as leeks, onions and Chinese cabbages of various types.

The cooking is oilier and saltier than that of the South. Garlic and soy are used sparingly.

Many of China's four million Moslems live in this region, in particular in Mongolia. During the thirteenth and fourteenth centuries China was ruled from Beijing (Peking) by the Moslem Mongols. This brought to North China barbecuing and slow stewing, rich seasonings and sauces, and a range of ingredients untypical of China, including lamb, mutton, goat, coriander and turmeric, and a heavy use of garlic and onion. Many Moslem Mongolian dishes are enjoyed there to this day.

But by far the greatest and most enduring influence on this region was brought about when the Imperial court of the Ming dynasty was established in Beijing in 1368. With it came the Mandarin style of cooking and spectacular dishes such as Peking Duck (see page 119).

The overthrow of the Ming dynastry in 1644 saw the departure of the court. Fortunately the excellent Pekinese cuisine developed at the height of the Ming dynasty lives on, and has become well known as *haute cuisine* in Chinese restaurants in the West.

The West

China's most westerly provinces are Szechwan (or Sichuan) and Yunnan, which share their borders with Tibet and Burma respectively. The food in this region is hot and spicy. Chilli, ginger, onion and garlic are used liberally and to great effect. This is perhaps not surprising when one considers that Burmese cuisine leans more to Indian than Chinese cooking in style.

Szechwan food is becoming increasingly widely known in the West, as more and more restaurants add this style of cooking to their menus.

The region is abundant in fruit, vegetables, pork and poultry. Although land-locked, there are many rivers and lakes and fish is popular. The climate is sub-tropical, and rice, wheat and corn grow in profusion. Sugar cane, tea, citrus fruits and mushrooms are also cultivated there. The region is celebrated for the Szechwan peppercorn (*fagara*) an aromatic spice unrelated to and not as hot as regular pepper (Szechwan pepper grows on the prickly ash tree).

It is the liberal use of chilli which either endears one to, or frightens one away from, Szechwan cooking. Chillies are cooked into dishes, sprinkled on top, served as dips or sauces and eaten raw as an accompaniment. Szechwan chillies are small and pungent, and deep red when ripe. They are so much a part of the diet of this region that it seems inconceivable that they only reached China in the sixteenth century following their discovery in the New World by the Portuguese.

CHINESE RESTAURANTS

In China

It is probably true to say that China invented the restaurant. Indeed there are more restaurants in China now than anywhere else on earth. It has always been so. A time traveller would not have found the streets of any Chinese city very different at the time of Marco Polo's visit in 1270 to those a thousand years earlier. The streets were thronged with people, shops, market stalls, tradesmen and food stalls and restaurants. The food they served was little different from that found in Chinatown today. Sweet aromas of garlic, soy and hoisin sauce wafted through the air tempting citizens to drool over menus offering a couple of hundred delicious dishes.

Two main kinds of restaurants did and still do exist – the Chiu Chia, or wine pavilions, where full meals are available, and the better known tea houses.

During the repressive years of Mao Tse-tung and his Cultural Revolution many ancient and well-established restaurants were forced to close. Since Mao's death and the reversal of austere policies, there has been a revival, much to the joy of the Chinese population.

In 1949 Peking had 10,000 snack bars and restaurants. By 1980 it had 500. They are on the increase again now, and one of the best is the *Quanjude Beijing Duck Restaurant.*

Chinese restaurants in China are not the cosy intimate affairs that they are in the West. They are large and well lit and like vast canteens. One of the most famous restaurants in China and certainly one of the largest is Canton's *Guanhzhou.* Established in 1906 it has four floors and serves 10,000 people each day.

In Britain and the West

The recent growth in popularity of Chinese food in Britain closely paralleled that of Indian. Both were spawned from the same basic marketing 'gap' in Britain as tastes, dining habits, spending power, mobility and, to an extent, class structure changed.

With the nineteenth century growth of Britain as an industrial power and sea-faring nation, Chinese sailors came to live in England, particularly in the ports of Liverpool and London. By the turn of the century this population was well established, and it was substantially increased during World War I. Dockland Chinese cafés became their eating haunts.

The Chinese sailors themselves came from the southern provinces of China. The type of food they wanted at their restaurants was straightforward Cantonese with no frills. Thus it was that the Chinese restaurant outside China evolved. In the early days Chinese ingredients were hard to get, but the resourceful Chinese restaurateurs soon overcame that obstacle.

In the early part of the twentieth century an adventurous restaurateur took the bold step of opening a Chinese restaurant in the West End of London. The clientele it aimed at were not native Chinese but native Londoners. But of course these were not any old Londoners, they were the 'toffs', the aristocracy and the wealthy. They were the cream of Edwardian society and the only people who could afford to eat in restaurants. The place was smart and expensive and, in the eyes of its patrons, a good place in which to be seen. Few had experienced the food of the mysterious Orient, and it was perceived to be amazingly exotic. The food it served was, of course, Cantonese.

That particular restaurant, which was in Shaftesbury Avenue, survived two world wars and the subsequent change of lifestyle and fashion, finally succumbing to closure in the 1970s. It was a real pioneer. For the first time it brought the taste of the East to the hub of the Empire – the world's most important and influential city. Gone it may be today but, like all great ancestors, its genes live on, in both its site, now at the heart of London's Chinatown, and its Cantonese menu. That restaurant's success guaranteed that its style and menu would be copied, and sure enough as time went by other Chinese restaurants opened in London and in other large British cities.

The real spread of the Chinese restaurant began to take hold in Britain during the late 1950s. It was slightly ahead of its curry counterpart. Much the same story was unfolding in other parts of the world, notably New York and San Francisco, where whole districts became identified as Chinatown. Later London, Birmingham and Manchester were to sprout their own China-towns, as did Amsterdam, Paris and Brussels.

By the early 1960s Chinese restaurants had begun to become established in the back streets of the bigger cities. They stayed open very late, were cheap and comfortable and served food which was at the time considered to be very exotic. It did not take long before curry houses followed suit. They too offered a new level of sophistication and exotica to a new generation of diners. Chinese restaurants were well ahead of Indian ones in terms of numbers and this remained the case until the present day when the curry houses caught up. There are now about 6,000 curry houses and 6,000 Chinese restaurants in Britain.

The early establishments quickly found out what diners wanted to eat Menus were evolved and honed, and over a decade or two perfected. Cooking techniques had to be fast and simple, wastage minimal and profits high. Kitchens were as small as possible to enable more seats to be got into the dining room, and labour, so plentiful in China and India, was kept to a minimum. Men, unskilled as cooks and often members of the proprietor's family, were roped in and either learned the skills of the restaurant or quit. Most learned. They lived over the shop and became fast and competent. Skills of waiting and language also had to be learned.

As with any cloning process, growth began slowly. A new place would open and the cook and waiter would transfer to the new place to receive a higher wage and status. Each would take his limited skills with him. The process of covering the nation had begun. Restaurant after restaurant opened. Decor, techniques, menu and cooking were identical. As each new town was reached its population soon discovered that they enjoyed the new very weird and unfamiliar foods. For the restaurant it was a well-tried formula.

By the late 1960s Chinese and Indian restaurants has proliferated to all the bigger towns and to many smaller ones. By the 1970s a new generation of diners had grown up with Chinese and Indian restaurants. Their expectations grew and they began to become bored with the standard menus. The Indian restaurants solved the problem by including Tandoori dishes – whilst on the Chinese front the Peking style of cooking made its appearance.

The restaurateurs also began to pioneer a new wave of 'up market' restaurants in prime and expensive high street sites. Out went the 'plastic' decor and the enormously lengthy menu. In came stylish decor and a short menu with better prepared items, which were more expensive. Customers were not only willing to pay for this sophistication, they demanded it.

Who could have foreseen just forty years ago the massive change in eating habits and dining out expectations that was to sweep across the nation. In 1950 it was extremely hard to obtain fresh garlic. Ginger was unknown, and the other fresh produce we now take for granted – beansprouts, Chinese leaves, baby sweetcorn and the rest – were equally unobtainable. The adventurous had to make forays to just one or two specialist emporia that existed in London. Now virtually everything you need is readily available at the local delicatessen, supermarket and greengrocer. Whereas a decade or so ago it would have been impractical to attempt to cook at home in the style of the Chinese restaurant, it is now quite feasible. And that is exactly what this book is for.

Chinatown

My first visit to a Chinatown came years after my first forays to Hong Kong and Singapore and it came as a huge pleasant surprise to me. It was in San Francisco in 1970 and I can remember to this day standing open mouthed at this magnificent fairy-land setting, looking for all the world as if it was out of the movies. But no, this wasn't Hollywood, it was San Francisco.

Everywhere there was colour. I entered Chinatown through a gigantic red, gold and green arch embellished with Chinese script and dragons. It was late at night and strings of Chinese lanterns illuminated the scene, delicately swaying in the gentle sea breeze. Hanging things tinkled and Chinese music was playing. But you could hardly hear it for the hustle and bustle everywhere. All the shops were open, their wares spread on the pavements as well as inside: gaudy knick-knacks, kites, paper dragons, face masks, Chinese crockery, chopsticks, books and newspapers in Chinese script. There were temples and teahouses, theatres and joss houses (shrines), and the famous Wax Museum. People were on the move everywhere. Many were Chinese, just going about their everyday life, and it was exciting. There was a lot of chatter in that clipped sing-song gutteral accent which every now and then makes you wonder if the participants are having a row.

But if there was one thing which transfixed me that first night, it was the aromas. Aromas from the Chinese grocers and from the Chinese restaurants. And everywhere you looked there were grocers and restaurants. In their windows hung red marinated ducks and Chinese sausages.

I'm familiar with it now, and I love it. San Francisco's Chinatown, with its population of 70,000, is the largest settlement of Chinese outside China. Those of New York, Chicago and Portland are nearly as big. The London Chinatown evolved during the 1970s. It has grown into several blocks of London's West End, bordered by Shaftesbury Avenue, Lisle Street, Wardour Street and Cambridge Circus. It too has its red embellished archways, its food stores, its restaurants and its smells. It too is exciting and busy at all hours. Indeed it has more than one restaurant open until 5 am which is very unusual for London. A visit to Chinatown and its restaurants is a must for anyone who enjoys Chinese food.

COOKING UTENSILS AND IMPLEMENTS

The wok

With a minimal range of utensils and implements, the most astonishing dishes are put together in village China.

The principal utensil is the wok. Although very few archeological remains exist today it is almost certain that the first wok evolved as a cast-iron or bronze cooking pot, many centuries BC.

The wok is the most versatile pan. It is a circular, round-bottomed steel pan with a single long handle. Sizes range from as little as 6 inches (15 cm) in diameter to as large as 24 inches (60 cm) in diameter. The average domestic wok should have a diameter of 12–14 inches (30–35 cm). Its gently sloping sides enable the cook to control both the evenness and temperature of the ingredients being cooked. The heat is greatest at the base of the pan and it becomes increasingly cooler as you move up the sides and away from the centre. By continually tossing and stirring the food the result is even, rapid cooking. Wok techniques are described on pages 21–2.

The wok has taken well to Western adaptation by the flattening of its base, making it suitable for use on an electric hob. Modern woks are made from pressed thin carbon steel and are a pleasure to cook with. The latest wok on the scene is an electric wok that heats itself. The temperature is controlled with a thermostat.

A new wok must be 'seasoned' by an initial washing to remove the factory protective coating of machine oil. It must then be wiped clean and reheated with a tablespoon of oil plus a teaspoon of salt. When it smokes, empty the oil out and wipe it with kitchen paper.

To clean a wok

A wok should never be scoured clean, for to do so would be to loose the blackened patina that builds up over time, and which is said to improve the flavour of the food being cooked. Indeed the Chinese say of a cook, 'the blacker the wok, the better the cook'.

It is true that a blackened wok looks the part, but (sacrilege!) I honestly cannot tell the difference between using a new well-scoured wok and my old well-blackened (and I'm sure less hygienic) one. However the best tool to use to clean a wok without scratching it or losing the patina is a Chinese wok brush. This is a fairly substantial item with a firm round handle and a number of stout bamboo 'bristles'. It cleans the wok effectively, but it then takes a fair bit of cleaning itself.

Items to use with a wok

The modern wok has a number of items of associated equipment. It has a steel stand on which to place it when off the stove. It has a well fitting domed lid. And it has a wire rack which fits inside for use when steaming. Also available is a wok spatula – a steel scraper whose blade is shaped to fit snugly to the curve of the wok. The Chinese use cooking chopsticks which are about 18 inches (45cm) long for moving items around in the wok. You may prefer to use a long-handled cooking spoon.

Two ladles are designed to work with the wok, one perforated, the other not. Also useful is a flat, round, wire strainer with a long handle, suitable for removing items which are being deep-fried in the wok.

Bamboo steaming baskets

These are essential if you wish to make steamed items. They are circular wooden cylinders with a criss-cross lattice of bamboo inside. They are designed to stack one above the other, the norm being three or four high. Different items for steaming are placed on each deck, and on top of the highest basket goes an attractive wooden lid. See page 97 for how to use.

Bamboo steaming baskets come in a variety of sizes, from as small as 6 inches (15 cm) to as large as 15 inches (37.5 cm). Probably the most useful size is about 8 inches (12 cm). Chrome steel steamers of the same design are also available.

Bird's nest strainer set

This is a very specialised item. It is a double set of strainers with long handles and a 'locking' device. See page 52 for how to make a Crispy Noodle Nest.

Cleaver

Every Chinese chef uses the cleaver as a multipurpose tool. As a cutter the blade is kept extremely sharp, and with its weight it can be used to cut items into the smallest shreds. The cleaver is also used as a hammer, and the side of the blade can be used as a crusher. Using a cleaver requires a fair bit of practice, and you will get equally good results using ordinary knives, so it is not an essential piece of kit.

Chopping board

The Chinese chopping board must be stout to cope with the weight of the cleaver. The traditional board is a round heavy piece of hardwood tree trunk, about 15 inches (37.5 cm) in diameter, 3 inches (7.5 cm) thick and very attractive.

Chopsticks

Chopsticks are used both for cooking and eating with. Once mastered, a Chinese meal undoubtedly tastes better using chopsticks. Most Chinese ones are made from wood or bone and have square tips. In the West a much wider range is available, including Japanese chopsticks which are pointed, shorter and more decorative.

COOKING TECHNIQUES

Stir-frying

Chinese cooking evolved, as we have seen, thousands of years ago. Even as far back as that, the country was highly populated and fuel and ingredients were scarce. Cooking took place over the wood fired embers of a central house fire and most cooking was designed to take place in a very few minutes. Probably the best known Chinese cooking technique which achieves the desired speed is the stir-fry.

Food is cut into thin bite-sized strips of approximately equal size. Oil is heated to a very high temperature then the food is placed into the pan, usually a wok (see page 19), and is continually kept on the move by tossing and stirring until it is cooked. Because the pieces of food are small their cooking time is fast, and because it is fast the food retains its colour, flavour and freshness. It must be served at once in order to retain these qualities.

Deep-frying

This is a technique used more by the restaurants than by authentic Chinese cooks. It is perfect for producing crispy items such as spring rolls and wontons.

Steaming

This is another very important Chinese cooking technique. Again it is done in the wok. A special wire rack is placed into the wok and water is poured in, leaving the rack standing clear. The water is brought to the boil and bamboo steaming baskets (see page 20) are placed on the rack. Items such as Wontons (see page 91) and pancakes (see page 121) are perfectly cooked in this way. See page 97 for more detailed instructions.

Other cooking techniques

Some Chinese dishes are slow cooked, stewed or casseroled. The time taken for this process can vary from an hour or two to overnight. Obvious examples are soups, stocks and certain meat dishes. If soy sauce is used in the stew, the dish is described as being red cooked. If it is absent, it is white cooked.

Barbecuing and grilling are not traditional Chinese cooking techniques but certain dishes can be cooked using these methods.

CUTTING UP THE INGREDIENTS

As Chinese food is eaten with chopsticks or soup spoons it follows that it is cut up into manageable bite-sized pieces before it is served. A few dishes are cut after they are cooked such as Peking duck. There are five main types of cut used for both vegetables and meat: chunks (*kuai*) or squares to a maximum of about $\frac{3}{4}$ inch (2 cm); small dice (*ding*) of between $\frac{1}{4}-\frac{1}{2}$ inch (6–12.5 mm); flat thin slices (*pian*); long narrow strips (*tiao*); and shreds (*si*). Other cuts can be utilised for more decorative occasions. These include cutting into squares, circles, stars, diamonds, grains of rice, indeed any shape which captures the imagination.

The convention is to cut all the ingredients which go to make up a particular dish to the same size and type of cut, whether meat or vegetable. This not only gives the dish a more attractive appearance, it ensures that seasonings impregnate the pieces more easily and that the cooking is even.

To shred meat or poultry

This is an important Chinese technique.
1. Choose the best cut of beef you can such as topside or rump steak and remove all unwanted matter. For poultry use only skinned and boned breast meat.
2. Cut the meat into slabs about 1 inch (2.5 cm) thick. Cut across the grain into strips about $\frac{1}{8}$ inch (3 mm) wide. Each strip will therefore be 1 inch (2.5 cm) thick by $\frac{1}{8}$ inch (3 mm) wide by a few inches (several centimetres) long. Trim the length to about $1\frac{1}{2}$ inches (3.75 cm) average.
3. Now cut the strips into shreds $\frac{1}{8}$ inch (3 mm) thick by $\frac{1}{8}$ inch (3 mm) wide by about $1\frac{1}{2}$ inches (3.75 cm) long.

Note: It is much easier to obtain perfect shreds by lightly freezing the slabs of meat in stage 1, then cutting with a sharp knife or cleaver.

To shred vegetables

1. Choose firm vegetables. Carrots, ginger, potatoes, moolis etc are all ideal.
2. Wash and peel the vegetables first. Cut each vegetable into blocks about $1\frac{1}{2}$ inches (3.75 cm) long. Then cut into slices $\frac{1}{8}$ inch (3 mm) thick. Cut again into juliennes (or matchsticks) $\frac{1}{8}$ inch (3 mm) thick by $\frac{1}{8}$ inch (3 mm) wide.

THE MEAL

The Chinese dinner table has, for me, glamour and excitement and a sense of expectation which no other culinary style even closely matches.

If you intend to serve Chinese food at home in style it will be worth investing in a matching set of Chinese table ware. A very wide selection is now available, usually in highly coloured porcelain, and it is relatively inexpensive.

Each place setting needs a soup bowl with matching flat shovel spoon (*charn*), and an eating bowl which is slightly smaller than the soup bowl. The eating bowl has a matching underplate. To complete the place setting you need a pair of chopsticks complete with a decorative piece to rest them on. Also on the table for general use should be some miniature bowls for sauces, perhaps some finger bowls, and a set of tea cups.

Matching serving dishes should be obtained. You will need flat oval plates for dry dishes and deeper oval or round plates for wet dishes. The serving plates are placed in the centre of the table and the diners should help themselves using their chopsticks to transfer the items from the serving plates to their own eating bowls. However I find it easier to use serving spoons for this otherwise tricky and messy business. For the really serious student of Chinese food, a table revolve (also called a lazy Susan or dumb waiter) is useful and it is a practical idea to put a food warmer on to the revolve or table. Inexpensive candle-powered versions are available and they greatly add to the sense of the occasion as well as keeping the food hot.

What to drink

Tea

Tea drinking is even more of a ritual in China than it is in England. It is made frequently and is served at any time of day or night. In certain regions of China, such as Canton, tea is served throughout every meal, whether or not alcohol is taken. It must be China tea, served hot and fresh, which means more than one brew during the meal, and it is served without milk or sugar.

In Chinese restaurants in the West you will most likely be served jasmin tea. It will be very weak but is delightfully fragrant and very refreshing.

Alcohol

There is a relatively substantial liquor industry in China and it is known that wine has been produced in China for at least 4,000 years.

Most of today's Chinese wines are made from fermented glutinous rice. The best variety of rice wine is called Shaoxing and it comes from the Zhejiang (Chekiang) province in Eastern China. Described as 'yellow' it has the colour of Scotch whisky and a rather sour taste. It is used for cooking and drinking. In its latter mode it should be served in porcelain mugs at approximately blood temperature (achieved by immersing the bottle in warm water). It is customary to add sugar to taste. Huadiao is a fortified version of Shaoxing. It too should be warmed and sweetened to taste.

China also has a beer producing industry. It is possible to obtain Chinese alcoholic beverages in specific outlets, and it does add a certain charm to the meal if you serve them. If you prefer, however, a more conventional drink may be served.

As with any spicy or highly flavoured food, fine wines are wasted, but most dry and medium-sweet white wines, and fuller bodied reds go well. Dry rosés are excellent with Chinese food, as are sparkling whites, and of course lager or non-alcoholic drinks are acceptable as well.

Menu suggestions

Selecting the menu is, I sometimes think, more exciting than cooking it. This is especially so for Chinese food.

Before you start, decide what theme you would like and how many courses you want. Then decide how many items you want per course. This is largely determined by the number of diners you're going to have. The more people who sit at the table, the greater the choice of dishes you can and should offer. The rule of thumb for the main course is to serve at least one different dish per person, plus a staple (rice or noodles). The more dishes the better, and everybody should get at least a taste of each dish.

The other important thing to remember is the Chinese concept of Yin-yang. This is explained on page 11. Each meal should be a perfect harmony and contrast of colours, textures and tastes. No main ingredient should be used more than once within a course. Each of these 10 menus, ranging from a simple home supper to an elaborate dinner party, shows the principles.

If the sheer number of items looks daunting, remember you can do a great deal of the preparation in advance, including some cooking. Certain items can be made ahead and frozen and any leftovers can also be frozen.

The recipes for all these dishes will be found by consulting the index. Each of the 8 colour photographs in this book shows a selection of dishes from some of the following menus.

A SIMPLE HOME MENU 1

Suggested number of diners 2–4

Spring Rolls

Fillet Steak Mandarin Style
Mushroom with Walnut
Steamed Beansprouts
Egg Fried Rice

Fruit or Ice cream

A SIMPLE HOME MENU 2

Suggested number of diners 2–4

Duck Soup

Pekinese Beef Stew
Stir-fry Vegetables
Shrimp Fried Rice
Crispy Deep-fried Rice Noodles

Fresh Fruit Salad

THE RESTAURANT FAVOURITE MENU 1
— • —

Suggested number of diners 4–6

Crispy Deep-fried Seaweed

———

Mini Spring Rolls
Sesame Chicken Toast Triangles
Beef Satay
Sweet and Sour Sauce

———

Pork Foo Yung (omelette)
Stir-fry Beef with Green Peppers and
Black Bean Sauce
Cantonese Lemon Chicken
Shrimp Fried Rice

———

Toffee Apples

THE RESTAURANT FAVOURITE MENU 2
— • —

Suggested number of diners 4–6

Prawn Crackers with Hoisin Sauce or
Plum Sauce

———

Mini Barbecue Spare Ribs
Deep Fried or Steamed Wontons

———

Chicken and Sweetcorn Soup

———

Sweet and Sour Pork
Prawn Chow-mein
Beef Chop Suey
Egg Fried Rice

———

Fresh Lychees

SEA TIME MENU
— • —

Suggested number of diners 4–6

Crispy Deep-fried Seaweed
Prawn Crackers

———

Shark's Fin Soup

———

Sesame Prawn Toast Fingers
Shanghai Crab Claws

———

Oyster Black Beans
Five-willow Fish
Sea-spicy Noodle Balls
Shrimp Fried Rice

———

Red Bean Curd Sweet Pancake

SZECHWAN HOT AND SPICY MENU
— · —

Suggested number of diners 4–6

Prawn Crackers with
Chilli Oil

———

Hot and Sour Soup

———

Stir-fry Beef or Pork with Szechwan Hot
Chilli
Szechwan Duck
Hot Spicy Chicken
Szechwan Chilli Prawns
Pe-tsai with Ginger and Nuts
Vinegared Chillies
Szechwan Chilli Sauce
Plain Rice

———

Eight Treasure Rice Pudding

VEGETARIAN MENU
— · —

Suggested number of diners 4–8

Crispy Noodle Nest filled with
Fried Cashew Nuts, served with
Peking Dip Sauce

———

Marbled Eggs
served on a pretty garnish of salad
and carved vegetables
Vegetable Spring Rolls

———

Sizzling Special Vegetables including
Lotus Roots
Stuffed Black Mushrooms
Stuffed Cucumber
Sour Plums with Cherry Tomatoes
and Celery
Silver Pin Noodles Topped with Crispy
Rice Noodles
Vegetable Fried Rice

———

Banana and/or Pineapple Fritters

CANTONESE SPECIAL MENU
— · —

Suggested number of diners 6–8

Deep-fried Cellophane Noodles

————————

Phoenix Cold Meat Platter
Pickled Vegetables

————————

Wonton Soup served in Melon Cups

————————

Sizzling Scallops
Stir-fry Duck with Pineapple and
Cashew Nuts
Three Meats with Spring Onion
Dragon's Teeth
Snow Pea Stir-fry
Char-siu and Ham Fried Rice

THE SHANGHAI DINNER PARTY
— · —

Suggested number of diners 8–12

Thin Pastry Crisps

————————

Chrysanthemum Fire Pot

————————

Shanghai Lion's Head
Yangtze Rabbit
Stir-fried Crab and Egg
Stir-fry Cucumber
Quail's Eggs and Lotus Nuts
Crispy Noodles
Duck Fried Rice

————————

Stuffed Chinese Pears

————————

Chinese Tea
Fortune Cookies

A PEKINESE IMPERIAL BANQUET
— · —

*A meal fit for the emperor and suitable for
a party or entertaining.*

Suggested number of diners 8–20

Treasure Bags (deep-fried wontons)
The Chicken and the Egg

————————

Peking Duck with Pancakes, Spring
Onions, Cucumber and Hoisin Sauce

————————

Tiger's Whiskers
Barbecued Pork
Peking Phoenix Emperor Prawns
Pekinese Drunken Chicken
Four-coloured Ball Vegetables
Pak-choi in Oyster Sauce
Black Bean Noodles
Eight Treasure Fried Rice

————————

Fresh Fruit Salad served in Melon Cups

————————

Chinese Tea
Almond Biscuits

CHAPTER 2

✛

BASIC FLAVOURINGS AND RECIPES

Chinese food is never served without at least one flavouring. As we have seen in Chapter 1, flavourings are fundamental to the Chinese philosophy of Yin and Yang, or the balance of nature. The four tastes are sweet, sour, bitter and salt, and we can accurately detect the presence of any one of these on different areas of the tongue. A further category is pungency or heat. This chapter concentrates on the definitions and descriptions of these tastes and their application to Chinese cookery.

The latter part of the chapter gives recipes for basic stocks, sauces and flavourings which are an essential background to the Chinese repertoire.

The stocks are quite concentrated and flavoursome and a spoon or two of one or other stock helps to give a tasty foundation to many of the recipes in this book.

Next comes the all-important range of pastes and sauces made from soya beans which make Chinese food so special in taste. They form a structural backdrop on which the other ingredients hang.

Then comes a selection of hot sauces based on chilli and ginger, which are used both as cooking flavourers and as table condiments.

There are three types of pickles which, sadly, rarely appear on the Chinese restaurant menu, but which are nevertheless superb table accompaniments to the rich fried main dishes.

Finally come three spicy mixtures. Spices do not figure very largely in Chinese cooking. Here are some interesting mixtures including the well known Chinese five-spice powder and the lesser known ten-spice powder and spicy salt.

There is an important point I should make about these basic recipes. All of them can be purchased as manufactured items. And there is a very wide range to choose from. Indeed the restaurants are, in the main, obliged to use proprietary brands because they lack the time to produce them themselves. You can choose whether to buy these items or whether to make them. The latter is more fun, and it is rewarding to get to grips with something mysterious like hoisin sauce or vintage master stock rather than to open a jar or use a stock cube.

My suggestion is that you try some of these recipes at least once to see if you prefer homemade to bought. If you don't then you can continue to use your favourite brands in the recipes in subsequent chapters with no loss of quality to the final result.

It may be unusual to mention ingredients which are *not* used in cooking, but there is one group which the Chinese detest and that is dairy products. You will not find, in any authentic recipe, reference to milk, cream, cheese or yoghurt. The only exception to this is the tiny minority Mongolian population who thrive on mare's milk.

GENERAL FLAVOURINGS

Most Chinese dishes establish a mouthwatering background taste by starting off their cooking with garlic and/or ginger and/or onion (usually spring onion or scallion). These can be used in any combination and quantity and are usually quickly stir-fried to impart their qualities to the oil in which they are fried.

Garlic

Garlic is believed to have originated in Siberia and the central Asian plain. This placed it in the path of the ancient traders who plied back and forth between the civilizations of the Middle East and China. And certainly the earliest records show that garlic was used in the cooking of both countries.

There are many garlic products on the market including dehydrated garlic flakes, garlic powder, garlic salt and garlic purée. Chinese restaurants have been known to use any or all of these. Flakes and purée are acceptable in flavour and texture. Powder is always detectable by its flavour, as is garlic salt. The real thing is the best, and it really is painless, if a bit odorous to prepare. Some recipes do, however, call for garlic powder.

There are two main ways that the Chinese prepare garlic. The first is to squash the whole clove with the side of the cleaver. The second is to dice, slice or shred it with the sharp end of the cleaver. Either way peel the clove first.

Not all the regions of China use garlic so some recipes do not include it. If you enjoy garlic you may wish to increase the quantities stated in the recipes.

Ginger

Ginger is a rhizome – a type of root which grows underground. It is native to Southern India, Indo-China and China itself, where some of the best ginger grows.

It is available in three forms: fresh, dehydrated and powdered. Only fresh should be used in Chinese cookery. It is now readily available in greengrocers and supermarkets, as it stays fresh for many months after it is harvested.

When selecting fresh ginger it is not immediately obvious whether it is fresh inside. The outside should have a beige or pinky-beige skin with a slight sheen. It should look plump and not withered. Where the root has been cut away from its stem or other parts of the root, there will be a dry scar and this is normal.

It is not possible to assess what the internal condition is like until the ginger is cut. It should be an even primrose-cream colour. It should be moist with no signs of blue (which is an indication of age and staleness) nor any dry spots. It should not be stringy, or tough.

To use ginger, you must first cut off any 'scars' and it is normal to peel off all the skin. A potato peeler makes the going easier. It is said that the skin makes the ginger taste bitter. I must say that I have not found that to be the case and it is certainly acceptable to leave some skin on if it is difficult to remove completely.

The main ways of preparing ginger after peeling it are to cut it into thin slices, shred it, or cut it into coarse or fine dice or cubes, or to make ginger juice (see page 43).

Ginger is quite hot and pungent and its use in Chinese cooking varies from region to region. If you adore the taste of ginger you may wish to step up the quantities specified in the recipes.

Spring onions

Onions are widely used in Chinese cooking. Most commonly they are a species of spring onion (scallion). Both the bulbs and the leaves are used to good effect, the latter providing colour as well as flavour.

Should you not have spring onions to hand it is perfectly acceptable to use ordinary onions in the recipes.

Spring onion tassels

Spring onions are also used as a garnish in the form of tassels. These are easily made. First cut the tops off the leaves leaving about $1-1\frac{1}{2}$ inches (2.5–3.75 cm) green leaves on the bulb. Make several slices through the leaves lengthways, down to the top of the bulb. Immerse in a bowl of cold water containing ice cubes for 30--60 minutes and the tassels will form. Drain and use immediately.

Chives

Several species of chive grow in China, including garlic chives. These are not readily available in the UK, but ordinary chives make a most attractive ingredient or garnish.

Coriander

Chinese cookery relies very minimally on herbs, indeed the only herb used frequently is fresh coriander leaf, also known as Chinese parsley. Coriander imparts a musky, slightly foetid aroma and taste which is not universally liked in the West. Indeed the word coriander is derived from the Greek word 'korus' meaning bedbug, which the reference books tell me smells the same.

Fresh coriander is now grown in Britain. It is also flown in daily from Cyprus, Egypt and Greece. Even so some greengrocers still refuse to stock it. You can track down a greengrocer who does stock it by finding out which one supplies the local Chinese (and Indian) restaurants. Whoever it is will supply coriander. Some supermarkets now stock it too.

It comes in rather large bunches and it will keep in the fridge for only a few days. It is the leaves only which you should use. You can open freeze any surplus, dry, in a tub (ensure there is no water clinging to it). If you shake it after its initial freeze the contents will separate and you will be able to use individual leaves which, although not quite as effective as fresh, nonetheless are better than none at all. After separating seal the container and return to the freezer for later use. If you cannot obtain fresh coriander you can use ordinary parsley. However, this will only enhance the appearance of the dish, it will not affect its flavour in the same way.

Spices

Compared with Indian and Middle Eastern cookery, relatively few spices are used to enhance the aroma, flavour or texture of food, or to give heat in Chinese cookery. The spices which are commonly used in Chinese cooking are listed below. Please refer to the Glossary for more detailed explanations of these spices.

Two spice combinations that are commonly used in Chinese cooking are five-spice powder and ten-spice (or taste) powder. See pages 44–5.

Aromatic spices
Cassia bark, cinnamon, cloves, fennel seeds, star anise, Szechwan pepper seeds.

Texture spices
Sesame seeds.

Heat giving spices
(Mostly used in the western provinces.) Chilli, mustard.

Less common spices
The following four spices are uncommon as far as Chinese cooking is concerned. They are green cardamom, coriander seeds, nutmeg and turmeric. They are used by the Mongolian and Moslem minorities mostly in the North of China.

MSG (*monosodium glutamate*)

This is known as *vetsin* or *mei chien* in Chinese. It is a white crystalline solid with virtually no taste or smell and is produced commercially from natural products. In the US it is made from gluten – a protein derived from wheat – while in the East soya bean protein is the main source. It is also produced by fermentation of molasses or sugar beet pulp by means of the bacteria *Micrococcus glutamicus*.

Medically it is used for treating hepatic coma, psychosis and even mental retardation.

What, though, can a white, odourless, tasteless substance do for food? It works as a flavour enhancer – in other words it accentuates other flavours in the food, probably by activating the taste buds in the mouth. It is recommended to be used with meat, fish, soups and vegetables but not with eggs, milk, fruit and sweets. This may be due to the fact that it activates only those taste buds capable of distinguishing savoury foods.

The use of MSG is a highly emotive subject. It is a food additive which enhances savoury flavours and like most additives it has side-effects. In the late 1960s a researcher reported that patients who had been frequenting Chinese restaurants complained of pains in the neck and chest. There is still some controversy over the exact cause of these pains but it is possible that a few people have an almost allergic sensitivity to monosodium glutamate, which is referred to as 'Chinese restaurant syndrome'.

Most Chinese restaurants do use MSG. I have chosen to omit its use throughout this book. However, if you do wish to use it, it is only necessary to do so in small quantities – but make sure you are using pure monosodium glutamate, as some brands contain salt as well. About $\frac{1}{2}$ teaspoon per pound (450 g) of meat or fish and $\frac{1}{2}$ teaspoon per quart (1.2 litres) of stock or per cupful of gravy are the recommended proportions. It can be added at any stage, but with meat it is best to rub it in before cooking. Don't be tempted to use more than necessary – it won't increase the flavour any more.

OTHER FLAVOURINGS

Fundamentally Chinese cooking relies on various flavouring liquids and sauces to add specific levels of sweet, savoury, sour and salt. These are examined here.

Chinese rice vinegars

To achieve an authentic flavour it is important to use Chinese vinegar where the recipe requires it. Made from rice, there are three main categories: black, red and white. Each has its own distinctive taste, and its use depends on the final colour you wish the dish to be. For example a white dish would require white vinegar to achieve the background tart taste. These vinegars are available from specialist stores and they last indefinitely.

Black rice vinegar

Very dark brown in colour and quite thick in texture.

Red rice vinegar

This is deep red in colour and is thinner in texture than black vinegar. It is generally sweeter in taste and can be used on its own as a dipping sauce.

White rice vinegar

This clear transparent vinegar is the mildest of the three types.

Chinese rice wines

Chinese rice wine is used for both cooking and drinking – which is fun for the cook!

Wine was certainly produced in China by 2000 BC and it has continued to be widely produced all over China ever since. Many wines are made from glutinous rice fermented with yeast and water. Other wines are made from maize and barley, for example *Gao-liang-jiu*. And *Mao-tai-jiu* is distilled from wheat and millet. No Chinese wines are made from the grape.

The best wine for cooking (not to mention drinking, see page 24) is Shaoxing from Eastern China. It is held in large earthenware vats for about a year before being strained and bottled. It is sometimes called yellow rice wine but is in fact pale brown in colour. It is mellow and sweetish in taste. It is slightly fortified at about 16° proof. *Hua-diao* is fortified Shaoxing wine and is even mellower.

Sherry makes an acceptable substitute for rice wine and where appropriate in the recipes I have specified the preferred type of sherry to be substituted.

China has a range of spirits, all very powerful at around 106° proof. Included are *Kwei-chiu-mou-tai* and *Fenhjui*. These are also referred to by the Chinese as wines, but beware their effects if you drink them!

Soy

The single most important ingredient in Chinese cookery is, of course, soy or to be more accurate the soya bean.

The Chinese have made this unremarkable and rather tasteless small round bean into something amazing. How this came about exactly is lost in the mists of time but many thousands of years ago the Chinese learned to use the soya bean. In its natural state it is small and pale cream in colour. When fermented it turns black, brown or yellow and is then soft enough to make into thick salty flavouring pastes and thin salty runny sauces of varying strengths. The ancients learned to compress the bean into cheese-like blocks (bean curd) which could be crumbled or cut and cooked. They also learned how to make it into a cooking oil and into a milk-like drink. They even use the unprocessed beans as a vegetable. In fact it is impossible to have a Chinese meal without including soy in one form or another.

Soy sauce

This is available in two main varieties. Thick or dark soy sauce is the thicker, darker and less salty of the two, and thin or light soy sauce is, obviously, thinner, lighter and more salty. Dark soy sauce gives a reddish brown colour to dishes while light soy sauce would be used when it is important for the food to be light in colour.

Custard powder

This is frequently used by Chinese restaurant chefs in place of cornflour. Custard powder is in fact just cornflour with additional flavourings (such as vanilla) and colour.

Cooking oils

The oils most commonly used in Chinese cooking are peanut (groundnut) oil, soy oil, sesame oil and sunflower oil. In Western China they use oil made from Szechwan peppers. In most of my Chinese recipes I use soy oil. Never use olive oil as this would give an excessively dominant flavour of olives that is unsuitable for Chinese dishes.

Stocks

Stocks are an important flavouring element in Chinese cooking. They intensify many dishes and also act as a vehicle for using up leftovers. The Chinese are very thrifty and they detest waste. The stock pot is their answer.

CHICKEN STOCK

Chinese cooking often requires the use of stock. The type most often used is purpose-made chicken stock. This is easy to make, and is an excellent way of using up spare chicken bones and meat.

$2\frac{1}{2}$ pints (1.5 litres) water
1 lb (450 g) chicken bones
2 oz (50 g) chicken meat

1. Select a pan large enough to hold the bones and water.

2. Bring the water to the boil in the pan. Add the bones and meat.

3. Cover and simmer for 2 hours or so by which time you should have about $1\frac{3}{4}$ pints (1 litre) of stock.

4. Strain, discarding the bones and meat, and cool. Keep in the fridge and use within 2 days or freeze in small moulds.

VEGETABLE STOCK

This tasty stock makes an alternative to chicken stock and greatly enhances the flavour of many Chinese dishes. Any vegetables and clean offcuts or vegetable trimmings can be used. The following recipe is just one suggestion.

5 pints (3 litres) water
8 oz (225 g) onion, peeled and chopped
6 cloves garlic, peeled and chopped
8 oz (225 g) carrot, chopped
4 oz (110 g) dried Chinese mushrooms

4 oz (110 g) Chinese leaves, shredded
2 tablespoons light soy sauce
1 tablespoon spicy salt
1 tablespoon ginger juice

1. Select a large saucepan with a capacity of at least 8 pints (4.5 litres) and bring the water to the boil in it.

2. Add the remaining ingredients, cover and simmer for 2 hours.

3. Strain, discarding the vegetable matter, and cool.

4. Keep in the fridge and use within 2 days or freeze in small moulds.

VINTAGE MASTER STOCK

The point of the vintage master stock is that once it is started, it is never allowed to run out, being topped up with any suitable bones and meat whenever they are available.

Vintage stocks are highly prized in China. I was told by a Chinese restaurateur that at his home in London he had a stock which had been brought from China by his grandfather some 50 years earlier, when he first came to London as a sailor. The actual start date of this stock he did not know, but the earlier the better, he declared.

A vintage master stock will keep for ever provided that it is strained regularly and boiled at least every other day.

Many international hotels run such a master stock system. Here is a traditional stock to start you off, using chicken, pork and duck.

5 pints (3 litres) water
1 cooked chicken carcass, skin
  removed
1 cooked duck carcass, skin removed

2 raw chicken drumsticks
2 raw pork chops, fat removed
1 tablespoon spicy salt

1. Select a large saucepan with a capacity of at least 8 pints (4.5 litres) and bring the water to the boil in it.

2. Break up the carcasses and drumsticks and chop up the raw meat. Put them into the boiling water with the spicy salt. Put the lid on.

3. When the water comes back to the boil, reduce the heat to give a low rolling simmer.

4. Check after $1\frac{1}{2}$ hours that all is well.

5. After 3 hours it will have reduced by about half. Remove from the heat. Strain, discarding the solid matter, and cool.

6. Store in the fridge in a suitable lidded container.

7. Ensure that it is either re-boiled every 2 days or that it is frozen.

8. Top up with any meat offcuts and sufficient water as required.

BLACK BEAN PASTE

This is another fundamental Chinese cooking flavouring which can be purchased in proprietary jars or cans. It is, however, easy to make using the ubiquitous soya bean. Made in the correct proportions this paste will keep for months, so I have given sufficient quantities to make a largish batch.

*8 oz (225 g) fermented black soya
  beans, canned or fresh
3 tablespoons caster sugar*

*2 tablespoons salt
1 tablespoon garlic powder
1 tablespoon ginger juice*

Simply put everything into a food processor. Pulse into a thick even paste and bottle.

Yellow Bean Paste

It is only the colour of this sauce which is different from the previous recipe. Simply substitute 8 oz (225 g) fermented yellow soya beans for the black ones.

Red Bean Paste

Again, this paste only differs from the two previous recipes in colour. Use 8 oz (225 g) of fermented red soya beans instead of the black ones.

HOISIN SAUCE

This sauce, also known as barbecue sauce, is widely used in the Chinese restaurant as a marinade sauce and cooking agent. It is sweet, thick, reddy-brown in colour and highly aromatic. Take a walk through any Chinatown and this is the delightful and distinctive fragrance that is all pervasive. It is also the traditional accompaniment to Peking duck.

There are many proprietary brands available and they vary widely in consistency, colour and flavour. It is not easy to capture the distinctive flavour, but here is a very successful recipe which I obtained from the Hong Kong Intercontinental Hotel.

It is a combination of many ingredients, each of which is strongly distinctive and individual, yet when they are combined the result is subtle and quite remarkable.

2 tablespoons red bean paste
2 tablespoons yellow bean paste
3 tablespoons Chinese yellow rice
  wine
2 tablespoons Chinese red or black rice
  vinegar
1 tablespoon caster sugar

2 cloves garlic, peeled and puréed
2 tablespoons cornflour
1 teaspoon custard powder
1 teaspoon Chinese five-spice powder
1 teaspoon chilli sauce (optional)
salt to taste

1. Mix all the ingredients together.

2. Pour into a bottle and leave in the fridge to marinate for 7 days before using.

3. It should then keep for several weeks in the fridge.

PLUM SAUCE

There are some very good plum sauces on the market, of which Amoy Gold is one of the best. It can be made quite easily at home. The best time to make a good batch is summer when plums are in season or you have a glut of plums from your garden. Plum sauce is the traditional accompaniment to crispy Szechwan Duck (see page 123).

1 lb (450g) red plums
4 fl oz (100 ml) Chinese white rice
  vinegar

2 tablespoons tomato ketchup
4 oz (110 g) granulated sugar

1. Chop and seed the plums.

2. Place the plums and the remaining ingredients in a stainless steel or enamel pan and simmer gently for half an hour or so, stirring occasionally.

3. Cool then purée in a food processor or blender. Pour into jars and seal with non-metallic lids.

CHILLI OIL

This clear red oil is frequently served in a tiny bowl as an accompaniment to the main meal. It is fiercely hot, and can only be made using fresh red chillies. This recipe makes a largish batch which can be bottled and kept indefinitely.

8 oz (225 g) fresh red chillies
$\frac{1}{2}$ pint (300 ml) soy or sunflower oil

1. Remove the stalks from the chillies, then slit them lengthways. Remove the seeds and any white pith.

2. Put them in a food processor and pulse into a purée. Alternatively finely chop them.

3. Heat the oil in a wok or frying pan to medium heat. Add the purée and stir-fry for 2–3 minutes, until the oil stops reddening.

4. Allow to cool then strain through muslin and store in an airtight bottle. Discard the chilli flesh (or use in the next recipe).

CHILLI AND GARLIC SAUCE

There is the archetypal chilli sauce which every restaurant produces on demand. Most don't actually make it – time is too pressing, and there are many proprietary makes available. However if you're feeling adventurous you can make your own with relative ease. This recipe makes sufficient to bottle and it can be kept indefinitely if made correctly.

1 lb (450 g) fresh red chillies
8 fl oz (250 ml) Chinese white rice
   vinegar
1 teaspoon salt

4 teaspoons garlic powder
2 teaspoons sugar
2 teaspoons cornflour

1. Remove the stalks from the chillies, then slit them lengthways. Remove the seeds and any white pith.

2. Soak the chillies overnight in the vinegar and salt.

3. Next day put them into a food processor and pulse into a fine purée.

4. Add the garlic powder, sugar and cornflour and enough water to give a pourable consistency. Pulse briefly to mix.

5. Bottle and use as required.

SZECHWAN CHILLI SAUCE

There are many proprietary Chinese chilli sauces available on the market. These vary markedly in flavour, consistency and heat strength – ranging from sweet to hot or even extra hot. This version is from Szechwan where the culinary tradition is for fairly hot food.

2 tablespoons vegetable oil
4 cloves garlic, peeled and finely
   chopped
1 inch (2.5 cm) cube fresh ginger,
   peeled and finely chopped
1 oz (25 g) onion, peeled and finely
   chopped
6 oz (175 g) fresh red chillies, de-
   stalked and finely chopped

2 fl oz (50 ml) Chinese red rice vinegar
1 tablespoon granulated sugar
2 tablespoons tomato ketchup
2 tablespoons Chinese yellow rice
   wine (optional)
2 teaspoons salt

1. Heat the oil in a wok or frying pan.

2. Add the garlic and ginger and stir-fry for 30 seconds, then add the onion and stir-fry for a further minute.

3. Add the chillies and the vinegar and simmer for 10 minutes. Add a little water as needed to prevent it drying up.

4. Add the remaining ingredients and simmer for 5 more minutes.

5. Remove from the heat and when cool process in a food processor or blender with sufficient water to make a smooth-textured sauce.

6. Bottle and use as required.

GREEN GINGER JUICE

Ginger juice is an ingredient encountered more often in authentic Chinese cooking rather than at the restaurant. Its purpose is to add ginger flavour without the pith.

The most convenient way of making ginger juice is in a blender (see below). Alternatively peel then grate the ginger and squeeze out the juice using your hand or a garlic press. Make a reasonable quantity and freeze it in an ice cube mould for later use. It is an excellent way to use up pieces of fresh ginger.

2–3 lb (900 g–1.3 kg) fresh ginger

1. Chop the ginger into smallish cubes, skin and all.

2. Put these into a blender and liquidize in batches until it is all used.

3. Strain and discard the 'pith'. Pour the liquid into an ice cube mould and freeze for 24–48 hours.

4. Break the cubes out of the mould and store in the freezer in an airtight box. Use as required.

Note: 1 cube is equivalent to 1 tablespoon of juice.

CHINESE FIVE-SPICE POWDER

Makes about 5oz (150 g)

Also known as *ng heung fun* or *wu hsiang fen*, this wonderfully aromatic combination of spices is used regularly in Chinese cooking, so it is worth making a reasonable quantity.

It can of course be purchased, but this homemade version, being roasted, is of much better quality than anything from a factory.

1 oz (30 g) stick of cinnamon
1 oz (30 g) cloves
1oz (30 g) fennel seeds

1 oz (30 g) star anise
1oz (30 g) Szechwan peppercorns

1. Heat the oven to 325°F/170°C/Gas 3.

2. Mix together these whole spices and spread them thinly and evenly on an oven tray.

3. Place the tray in the hot oven. Remove after 10 minutes.

4. Allow to cool completely, then grind to a fine powder in a coffee grinder, electric spice mill or with a mortar and pestle.

5. Keep in an airtight jar. Use within 6 months for maximum flavour.

CHINESE TEN-SPICE POWDER

Makes about 5 oz (150 g)

Also called Chinese Taste Powder, *wei fen* or *baa kuk tee*, this combination of flavourings is used as a sprinkler or as a dunking condiment. You can vary the proportions of the ingredients to suit your taste, if you wish.

2 oz (50 g) Chinese five-spice powder
2 oz (50 g) sea salt, finely ground
1 oz (25 g) caster sugar
1 teaspoon (5 g) liquorice powder

$\frac{2}{3}$oz (20 g) Szechwan peppercorns,
*   roasted (see previous recipe) and*
*   finely ground*
1 teaspoon dried chives

1. Mix all the ingredients together thoroughly.

2. Store in an airtight jar. Use within 6 months for maximum flavour.

PRAWN POWDER

This can be purchased from Chinese delicatessens, or it can be made at home. The resourceful Chinese use discarded prawn shells to add bulk to ground dried prawns, and the result is very tasty. You can omit the shells if you prefer.

1 cupful prawn shells
1 cupful dehydrated (dried) prawns

1. Heat the oven to 325°F/170°C/Gas 3.

2. Spread the shells and prawns out on an oven tray. Place into the oven and roast for 10–15 minutes.

3. Remove and allow to cool completely.

4. Grind the mixture in an electric grinder or spice mill.

5. Store in an airtight jar and use as required. It will keep for several months.

SPICY SALT

Makes about $2\frac{1}{2}$ oz (70 g)

Use this condiment as a sprinkler whenever you wish to salt Chinese food. It is essential that the wok is completely dry before you begin the stir-frying.

2 oz (50 g) sea salt
1 tablespoon Szechwan peppercorns, whole

1 teaspoon Chinese five-spice powder

1. Heat a dry wok or frying pan to medium heat.

2. Add the peppercorns and stir-fry for a minute or so.

3. Add the salt and stir-fry for a further minute.

4. Allow to cool then add the five-spice powder.

5. Grind in a coffee grinder or with a mortar and pestle.

6. Store in an airtight jar.

PICKLED GINGER

Makes 2 medium-sized jars

This age-old traditional pickle has been made in China since before recorded history. There are many proprietary brands available, but it is so easy to make that it really is a must. All you need is patience to allow it to mature for a month before you use it.

1 lb (450 g) fresh ginger
1 pint (600 ml) Chinese white rice
   vinegar

2 tablespoons caster sugar
1 tablespoon spicy salt

1. Peel the ginger and cut it into strips about 2 inches (5 cm) by $\frac{1}{4}$ inch (6 mm).

2. Place the vinegar in a pan and bring to the boil. Add the sugar. When the sugar has dissolved, remove from the heat and allow the liquid to cool. Add the salt.

3. Place the strips of ginger in clean jars and cover with the liquid.

4. Seal with non-metallic lids and store in a cool dark place. Leave for a month before using but check after 3 or 4 days to see if the vinegar needs topping up.

VINEGARED CHILLIES

Most Chinese people don't relish 'heat'. The exception are those of the Western provinces of Szechwan and Yunnan where they like things very 'hot' indeed.

Use tiny red or green chillies if you can get them for this fiery pickle.

1 lb (450 g) tiny red or green chillies
1 tablespoon spicy salt

1 pint (600 ml) Chinese white rice
   vinegar

1. Cut the stalks off the chillies and discard. Spread the chillies out on a chopping board and sprinkle the salt over them. Leave for a couple of hours.

2. Place the chillies in clean jars and cover with the vinegar.

3. Seal with non-metallic lids and store in a cool dark place. Leave for a month before using but check after 3 or 4 days to see if the vinegar needs topping up.

PICKLED VEGETABLES

Every household in China makes its own pickle. There are innumerable recipes and any combination of vegetables can be used – this recipe is just one suggestion. The pickle itself contrasts very well with all Chinese food and in particular stir-fries. As with the previous two pickles, this recipe makes a reasonable batch which can be bottled and stored.

Vegetables

8 oz (225 g) pak-choi or spinach,
coarsely shredded
8 oz (225 g) Chinese leaves, coarsely
shredded
8 oz (225 g) mangetout
2–4 fresh green chillies (optional)
8 oz (225 g) carrot, coarsely chopped
4 oz (110 g) rhubarb, coarsely
chopped
4–8 cloves garlic, peeled and finely
chopped
2 oz (50 g) fresh ginger, peeled and
finely chopped

Pickling sauce

2 pints (1.2 litres) water
3 fl oz (75 ml) Chinese white rice
vinegar
3 fl oz (75 ml) Chinese yellow rice
wine
2 tablespoons sugar
1 tablespoon hoisin sauce
1 tablespoon tomato ketchup
1 tablespoon salt

1. Mix the pickling sauce ingredients together.

2. Mix all the vegetables together in a bowl.

3. Pack the vegetables into jars and top up to the brim with the pickling sauce.

4. Leave for 2–3 days and then check that all is well, topping up with extra pickling sauce or vinegar if necessary. You can eat the pickle then and there or leave it to mature further. The longer it is left the softer the vegetables become.

CHAPTER 3

APPETISERS

For entertaining or special occasions the setting for a Chinese meal should be glamorous and exciting, as in the top class restaurants. The gorgeous colours of the crockery, napkins and table cloth, complete with sets of chopsticks, lead to a sense of anticipation for the meal to come. Add candlelight and cut-glass wine goblets or china teacups and expectations are considerably heightened.

What can tempt the appetite further than some crisp and tasty appetisers which you can place on the table as soon as you want the proceedings to begin? This chapter contains a typical selection of restaurant nibbles, plus a recipe for a dip sauce to accompany them.

Prawn Crackers and Crispy Deep-fried Seaweed are well known in the Chinese restaurants of the West, and both are easy to recreate at home. Thin Pastry Crisps are made from spring roll pastry and are delicious served with Peking Dip Sauce, while Crispy Noodle Nests and Fried Cashew Nuts have other uses in Chinese cooking in addition to their role as appetisers.

PRAWN CRACKERS

It would be inconceivable to have a Chinese meal without prawn crackers. Those light, crunchy, tasty crisps which precede the meal are quite unique. But what are they? They are, in fact, a mixture of rice flour and shrimp powder which is moulded and dried before being packaged into sachets or boxes and sold to shops and restaurants. They are available in this form from Chinese supermarkets and simply require deep-frying at home.

1. Allow about 6–8 pieces per diner. Place them into a deep-fryer preheated to 375°F/190°C (chip-frying temperature). They double or even treble in size so don't overload the fryer. After an initial whoosh and expansion, give them about 10 seconds more cooking, then remove from the oil with tongs and shake off the excess oil.

2. Place on absorbent kitchen paper and leave to drain and crisp up.

3. Serve warm or cold. They will keep in an airtight tin for some time.

CRISPY DEEP-FRIED SEAWEED

Serves 4

This is a superb appetiser which goes very well with prawn crackers and some hoisin dip before the meal begins in earnest. But what of the dish itself? The first thing to say is that it is not an authentic Chinese dish. The second is that it is not seaweed! It is, however, absolutely delicious, being very finely shredded cabbage, its dark-green leaves being firm and dry enough to deep-fry. Sprinkled with prawn powder the result is amazing.

half a pak-choi (Chinese cabbage)
oil for deep-frying
prawn powder for sprinkling

1. Cut the green leaves off the pak-choi, leaving the white stalks for other use.

2. Very finely shred the green leaves.

3. Heat the deep fryer to 375°F/190°C (chip-frying temperature). Do not use the basket.

4. Place a handful of the shreds into the deep-fryer. They will whoosh up and cook at once (within 10 seconds).

5. Remove with a large hand strainer and strain. Shake the excess oil off and place on kitchen paper to drain.

6. Repeat stages 5 and 6 with the remaining shreds of pak-choi. When all the shreds are cooked, place into a warmer or low oven until you are ready to serve. They will go crispy.

7. Serve hot sprinkled with the prawn powder.

THIN PASTRY CRISPS

Nothing could be simpler than this appetiser which I met in London's Chinatown. Eat with a Chinese dip such as Peking Dip Sauce (see page 53).

4 sheets spring roll pastry

1. Heat the deep-fryer to 375°F/190°C (chip-frying temperature).

2. Cut the pastry into thin strips about ½ inch (1.25 cm) wide. Either cut them again to create rectangles about 2 inches (5 cm) long, or carefully tie the strips into bows.

3. Gently lower them into the deep-fryer. They will cook instantly. Remove after 5 seconds or so and place on absorbent kitchen paper to drain off excess oil and to crisp up. Serve hot or cold.

CRISPY NOODLE NEST

Makes 4 nests

Noodle nests or baskets are one of the masterpieces of Chinese food presentation. They look absolutely gorgeous and can be served as nibbles or used to hold starter ingredients or as the centre-piece of the main course. They are also used to make 'mock' bird's nest soup.

The photograph opposite page 128 shows the idea. Any type of noodle can be used: rice vermicelli make white nests while egg noodles make golden nests.

The noodles must first be boiled, then allowed to dry. To create the nest two all-metal strainers are needed, one slightly smaller than the other. I use one with a diameter of 5 inches (12.5 cm) and another with a diameter of 4 inches (10 cm). Alternatively special bird's nest strainer sets are available.

Nests can be made well in advance and stored, like biscuits, in airtight containers. They can then be warmed and re-crisped in a low oven. The nests can also be frozen.

7 oz (200 g) egg noodles
sufficient vegetable oil for deep frying
in a large wok

1. Boil 3 pints (1.8 litres) water in a 5-pint (3-litre) saucepan. Cook the noodles as the packet directs. Strain and cool under the cold tap. Strain again.

2. Place the noodles on absorbent kitchen paper, cover and leave overnight to dry.

3. Next day, heat enough oil in a large wok to enable you to immerse the strainers.

4. Divide the noodles into four. Oil both strainers by immersing them in the oil.

5. Press one batch of noodles into the larger strainer. Press the second strainer down on to the noodles.

6. Holding both handles together, lower the strainers into the oil. Cook for about 3 minutes.

7. Remove the strainers from the wok, shaking off excess oil. Carefully remove the smaller strainer from inside the larger one, then, using a knife if necessary, knock out the nest from the bottom strainer.

8. Repeat stages 5, 6 and 7 to make three more nests.

FRIED CASHEW NUTS

Most people enjoy nuts as an appetiser, and the cashew features prominently in Chinese cooking (see pages 105 and 149). In this method the nuts can be cooked well in advance and stored in an airtight container until needed. Try nibbling these with Chinese rice wine.

5 fl oz (150 ml) sesame oil
1 lb 2 oz (500 g) raw shelled cashew nuts

1 tablespoon spicy salt
1 tablespoon sugar

1. Heat the oil in a wok or frying pan.

2. Carefully place the nuts in and stir-fry for about 4–5 minutes. Watch out that they don't burn – keep them moving about frequently.

3. Strain the nuts from the oil (which can be used for subsequent cooking).

4. Put the nuts into an airtight container while they are still warm. Sprinkle over the spicy salt and sugar and put the lid on. Shake well. Serve when wanted.

PEKING DIP SAUCE

This dip sauce goes well with all the crispy appetisers in this chapter. It should be about the consistency of tomato ketchup. This is, of course, a restaurant invention, and it does not appear universally. I did meet one version delightfully entitled 'drunken dip' and it is this one I have endeavoured to reproduce here. This recipe makes enough for several uses, so it should be stored in a jar until needed.

6 tablespoons thick hoisin sauce
6 tablespoons Chinese yellow rice wine

1 teaspoon cornflour
2 teaspoons caster sugar

1. Mix all the ingredients together.

2. Pour into an airtight jar and use as required.

CHAPTER 4

❖

SOUPS AND STARTERS

Soup appears at virtually every meal in China, often because no other form of beverage will be taken during the meal. For a simple meal the soup will contain a high proportion of solid ingredients and it will be served as a meal in its own right with rice as an accompaniment.

Normally, however, soup forms part of a meal and in China it is rarely served first but often comes between courses, to cleanse the palate. Only if a soup is of outstanding appearance or contains an exceptional ingredient is it served first and on its own. Soup can even come at the end of a meal and it is common household practice to put items left over from the main dishes into a hotpot for an instant end-of-meal soup. An attractive way to serve soup is in carved melon bowls (see page 177).

Starters do not appear in the traditional Chinese meal in quite the same way they do for us in the West. At a Chinese meal at home, any of the dishes in this chapter could appear as part of the single course that Chinese families serve.

At the banquet or formal dinner party, where a great many courses might be served, they might appear at any time, on their own, throughout the meal.

Our Chinese restaurants like us to have starters, just as much as we do, and my choice of eleven is a representative and very varied selection culled from many restaurant menus. Most are hot, the exceptions being the highly decorative Phoenix Cold Meat Platter and the Marbled Eggs. Some are well known, for example Mini Spring Rolls and Mini Spare Ribs. The most intriguing is the Chrysanthemum Fire Pot which is a wonderful dish for entertaining, encouraging laughter and chatter because the diners cook their own ingredients on the special stove set up at the table.

Wontons are often served as starters or light meals in the Chinese restaurant and you will find these in Chapter 5, Restaurant Favourites.

CHICKEN NOODLE SOUP

Serves 4

This simple soup is one of the most popular Chinese restaurant soups.

$1\frac{3}{4}$ pints (1 litre) chicken stock
8 oz (225 g) chicken meat, skinned
  and finely chopped
4 spring onions, finely chopped
1 inch (2.5 cm) cube fresh ginger,
  peeled
  and finely chopped
1 teaspoon sesame oil

4 oz (110 g) egg noodles
1 oz (25 g) ham, finely chopped
  (optional)
1 tablespoon chopped fresh coriander
spicy salt to taste
finely chopped fresh parsley or
  spring onion leaves for garnish

1. Bring the stock to the boil in a 5-pint (3-litre) saucepan.

2. Add the chicken pieces, the spring onions, ginger and oil and simmer for 10 minutes.

3. Add the noodles, the optional ham and fresh coriander. Bring to the boil, simmer, then reduce the heat for about 3–4 minutes. Season to taste with spicy salt.

4. Pour into individual serving bowls, garnish with the parsley and serve piping hot.

Note: If the stock is not concentrated enough add one or two chicken stock cubes at stage 1 to give a more intense flavour.

Chicken and Sweetcorn Soup

This is a simple variation of the previous recipe, substituting 4 oz (110 g) fresh or frozen sweetcorn (thawed) for the noodles.

Chicken and White Mushroom Soup

This is another simple variation of Chicken Noodle Soup, substituting 4 oz (110 g) chopped white mushrooms for the noodles.

Chicken and Asparagus Soup

This final variation on the chicken soup theme uses asparagus and can therefore be regarded as an attractive, luxury soup, suitable for a dinner party. Simply substitute 4 oz (110 g) canned or fresh asparagus, carefully cut into smallish pieces, for the noodles.

If using fresh asparagus, which of course is superior in every way to canned, cut off the pithy bases of the stems and simmer the soup until the asparagus chunks are tender.

HOT AND SOUR SOUP

Serves 4

This traditional soup recipe comes from China's most westerly province, Yunnan, which shares its border with Burma. The cooking here is quite spicy and hot, reflecting the tastes of its neighbour. This soup has become a favourite in the Chinese restaurants of the West.

1¾ pints (1 litre) chicken stock
2 oz (50 g) tofu, finely chopped (optional)
1 oz (25 g) dried Chinese mushrooms, reconstituted (see page 146) and chopped
4 oz (110 g) ham, shredded
1 oz (25 g) beansprouts
1 teaspoon cornflour, mixed with water to form a paste
2 tablespoons Chinese red rice vinegar
1 teaspoon dark soy sauce
2 spring onions, finely chopped

1 clove garlic, peeled and finely chopped
2–6 fresh red or green chillies, chopped
1 teaspoon brown sugar
1 tablespoon sesame oil
2 eggs, beaten
3 tablespoons Chinese yellow rice wine or sweetish table wine (optional)
spicy salt to taste
4 spring onion tassels (see page 31) for garnish

1. Bring the stock to the boil in a large saucepan.

2. Add all the remaining ingredients *except* the eggs, wine, salt and spring onion tassels and simmer for 5 minutes.

3. Trickle in the beaten egg and add the optional wine and the spicy salt to taste.

4. Pour into serving bowls, garnish with spring onion tassels and serve piping hot.

Note: If the stock is not concentrated enough add one or two chicken stock cubes at stage 1 to give a more intense flavour.

DUCK SOUP

Serves 4

I came across this recipe in a Chinese restaurant near Hollywood. The menu made great play of the Marx brothers film of the same name. Indeed every single dish on the menu had some link with a movie star, no matter how tenuous. Duck soup is, however, a traditional Chinese dish which makes thrifty use of leftover duck bones.

$1\frac{3}{4}$ *pints (1 litre) chicken, vegetable or vintage master stock*

bones and remaining meat from 1 leftover duck carcass (including the offal)

2 oz (50 g) duck breastmeat, skinned and chopped

2 oz (50 g) onion, peeled and chopped

1 clove garlic, peeled and sliced

1 inch (2.5 cm) cube fresh ginger, peeled and sliced

1 tablespoon sesame oil (optional)

1 teaspoon hoisin sauce

1 teaspoon plum sauce

1 teaspoon light soy sauce

1 teaspoon brown sugar

1 teaspoon Chinese red rice vinegar

2–4 tablespoons Chinese yellow rice wine or sweet table wine (optional)

spicy salt to taste

1 tablespoon chopped fresh coriander

1. Bring the stock to the boil in a 5-pint (3-litre) saucepan.

2. Add the duck bones and offal. Simmer uncovered for 30 minutes. Strain and discard the solids.

3. Return the liquid to the saucepan and bring back to the boil.

4. Add all the remaining ingredients *except* the wine, salt and coriander.

5. Simmer for about 20 minutes. Add the optional wine and the spicy salt to taste.

6. Serve as soon as it is piping hot, garnished with fresh coriander.

BIRD'S NEST SOUP

Serves 4

In ancient China they must have tested everything to see if it was edible. Every kind of bird from large to small was consumed. It was logical, one supposes, that their nests were tried as well!

Amazingly the nest of one bird, a kind of swallow, is not made from twigs and straw but from a kind of spittle which hardens on contact with the air to form a strong, firm, densely latticed nest. These nests are quite small and must be thoroughly boiled to clean them, then dried. They are available in this form from Chinese grocers. The more usual and acceptable 'bird's nests', however, are made from noodles. For this soup make them no bigger than 3 inches (7.5 cm) in diameter. Allow one per diner.

$1\frac{3}{4}$ *pints (1 litre) chicken, vegetable or vintage master stock*
2 cloves garlic, peeled and sliced
1 inch (2.5 cm) cube fresh ginger, peeled and shredded
2 oz (50 g) onion, peeled and finely shredded
1 oz (25 g) carrot, grated
1 oz (25 g) celery, finely chopped
1 tablespoon light soy sauce

1 oz (25 g) watercress
2 oz (50 g) pak-choi or spinach
4 tablespoons Chinese yellow rice wine or dry sherry (optional)
4 quail's eggs, soft boiled for 2 minutes, then shelled
spicy salt to taste
4 crispy noodle nests (see page 52)
chopped spring onion tops for garnish

1. Bring the stock to the boil in a 5-pint (3-litre) saucepan.

2. Add the garlic, ginger, onion, carrot, celery and soy sauce. Simmer for about 5 minutes.

3. Add the watercress, pak-choi and the optional wine.

4. Add the quail's eggs and season with spicy salt to taste. Return the soup to the boil.

5. Place one nest in each serving bowl and pour the soup in on top. Ensure the eggs are equally distributed between the bowls. Garnish with chopped spring onion leaves. Serve piping hot.

CRAB CREAM SOUP

Serves 4

This rich soup is based on a recipe from China's eastern seaboard city of Shanghai. The crabs of the East China Sea are renowned for their flavour. They are not easily obtained in the West, so the restaurants here use cooked frozen crab meat to prepare this delicious soup.

$1\frac{3}{4}$ *pints (1 litre) chicken, vegetable or*
  vintage master stock
6 spring onions and leaves, sliced
  diagonally
$\frac{1}{2}$ *red pepper, thinly sliced*
1 teaspoon hoisin sauce

spicy salt to taste
4 oz (50 g) white crab meat, thawed
  if frozen
4 oz (50 g) brown crab meat, thawed
  if frozen
2 fl oz (50 ml) single cream

1. Bring the stock to the boil in a 5-pint (3-litre) saucepan.

2. Add the sliced spring onions and leaves, reserving a few leaves for garnish. Add the pepper, hoisin sauce and spicy salt. Simmer for 3–4 minutes.

3. Add the crab meat and the cream and when the soup simmers again it is ready to serve. Finely chop the reserved spring onion leaves and use to garnish the soup.

WONTON SOUP

Serves 4

This highly presentable soup uses that delightful Chinese invention, the wonton. These are tiny pastry shapes wrapped around a minced filling. The full description of wontons is on pages 91–9 . For this soup you will have to make the wontons smaller than usual. Wontons can be made in bulk and frozen so that you always have some to hand for making this soup.

$1\frac{3}{4}$ pints (1 litre) chicken, vegetable or
    vintage master stock
2 oz (50 g) onion, peeled, sliced and
    shredded
2 cloves garlic, peeled and finely sliced
$\frac{1}{2}$ inch (1.25 cm) cube fresh ginger,
    peeled and shredded
1 teaspoon sesame oil
1 tablespoon dark soy sauce

1 teaspoon brown sugar
1 teaspoon Chinese rice vinegar or
    distilled malt vinegar
spicy salt to taste
16 uncooked wontons, stuffing of your
    choice (see pages 91–6)
1 tablespoon finely chopped fresh
    parsley

1. Bring the stock to the boil in a 5-pint (3-litre) saucepan.

2. Add all the ingredients *except* the wontons and parsley and simmer for 5 minutes.

3. Add the wontons and simmer for a further 5 minutes.

4. Pour the soup into individual serving bowls, ensuring that the wontons are equally distributed. Garnish with the parsley and serve straight away.

HUNANESE FISH CHOWDER

Serves 4

I encountered this thick hearty soup in a Chinese restaurant in Sydney. The chatty chef-proprietor told me that he originally came from the central Chinese province of Hunan and had lived on the banks of the Yangtze river where the fish were plump and plentiful. Before settling in Australia, he had been in America – the home of the chowder. This soup was his invention.

8 oz (225 g) cod steaks, filleted and skinned
4 oz (110 g) prawns, thawed if frozen and peeled
2 cloves garlic, peeled and crushed
1¾ pints (1 litre) chicken, vegetable or vintage master stock
1 tablespoon light vegetable oil
2 tablespoon dark soy sauce

2 teaspoons brown sugar
2 teaspoons Chinese rice vinegar or distilled malt vinegar
3 tablespoons Chinese yellow rice wine or sweet sherry
spicy salt to taste
1 tablespoon finely chopped fresh parsley for garnish

1. Hand mash the fish, prawns and garlic into a mince-like texture or coarse purée.

2. Heat the stock in a 5-pint (3-litre) saucepan.

3. Add the purée to the stock and bring to the simmer. Add the oil, soy sauce, sugar and vinegar and simmer for about 10 minutes.

4. Add the rice wine and, if you wish, thin the chowder with water until you obtain the texture of your choice. Season to taste with spicy salt.

5. Serve hot, garnished with the finely chopped parsley.

SHARK'S FIN SOUP

Serves 4

Shark's fin soup is one of China's more celebrated dishes. Originally it was a simple fisherman's dish devised in coastal China thousands of years ago. The shark's fin itself is rather tasteless and has a soft, fleshy texture. It is available dried or canned. The former requires lengthy simmering to reconstitute it while the latter just needs draining and rinsing thoroughly. The liquid from the can may be added to the stock, but taste it first to see if you like it.

$1\frac{3}{4}$ *pints (1 litre) chicken or vintage master stock*
7–8 oz (200–225 g) can shark's fin, drained then rinsed thoroughly
8 oz (225 g) raw chicken breast meat, skinned and shredded
4 dried Chinese mushrooms, reconstituted (see page 146)
2 oz (50 g) ham, shredded
1 teaspoon cornflour

1 tablespoon Chinese white rice vinegar or white wine vinegar
1 tablespoon light soy sauce
1 teaspoon brown sugar
spicy salt to taste
2 tablespoons Chinese yellow rice wine or sweet sherry
1 tablespoon finely chopped fresh coriander for garnish

1. Bring the stock to the boil in a 5-pint (3-litre) saucepan, together with the liquid from the canned shark's fin, if you like the taste.

2. Add the shark's fin, chicken meat, mushrooms and ham and simmer for 10 minutes.

3. Mix the cornflour with the vinegar and add to the stock together with the soy sauce and sugar. Add spicy salt to taste. Bring back to simmering point.

4. Add the rice wine and serve when it is piping hot, garnishing with the fresh coriander.

SHADOW OF BUTTERFLY

Serves 4

Also known as prawn butterfly, this dish of deep-fried tiger or giant king prawns gets its name from the shape formed when the prawns are split down the front, opened out and flattened.

4 tiger or giant king prawns, thawed,
   if frozen

Batter
3 tablespoons cornflour
2 tablespoons plain flour
3 egg yolks
1 teaspoon spicy salt

Garnish
shredded lettuce
mustard and cress

1. Make the batter first by beating together the flours, egg yolks and salt. Set aside.

2. Heat the deep-fryer to 375°F/190°C (chip-frying temperature).

3. Peel the prawns, leaving the tails on. Cut lightly along the back of each with the point of a sharp knife and remove the vein. Wash the prawns thoroughly and pat dry on kitchen paper.

4. Take one prawn and split open by cutting down its front, but be careful not to cut right through the flesh. Place the prawn on a work surface and gently press it flat to make the butterfly shape.

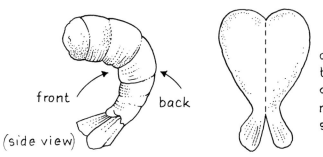

front

back

(side view)

after cutting down the front, open out and press flat to make the butterfly shape

5. Repeat stage 4 with the remaining 3 prawns.

6. Coat each prawn in batter and drop into the deep-fryer. Cook for about 8–10 minutes then remove and drain on absorbent kitchen paper.

7. Serve hot on a bed of shredded lettuce garnished with mustard and cress.

SESAME PRAWN TOAST FINGERS

Makes 16 fingers

This is a straightforward starter for those who enjoy seafood.

8 oz (225 g) raw prawns, thawed if
  frozen and peeled
1 tablespoon chopped fresh coriander
1 spring onion, chopped
1 clove garlic, peeled and chopped

2 teaspoons cornflour
½ teaspoon spicy salt
1 teaspoon sesame oil
2 slices dry white bread
1 tablespoon sesame seeds

1. Put the prawns, coriander, spring onion, garlic, cornflour, spicy salt and oil in a food processor. Pulse to make a purée.

2. Spread the purée evenly over the two slices of bread. Sprinkle the sesame seeds over the purée and gently press them into place.

3. Heat the deep-fryer to 375°F/190°C (chip-frying temperature) and fry the two slices, one at a time, for about 5 minutes.

4. Remove from the fryer, shake off excess oil and cut each slice into 8 fingers. Alternatively cut into small bite-sized squares. Serve hot.

Sesame Chicken Toast Triangles

This is a variation of the previous recipe, using 8 oz (225 g) raw chicken breast meat, skinned and cut into strips, in place of the prawns. The deep-fried toasts are cut into 16 triangles rather than fingers.

Opposite THE FAVOURITE RESTAURANT MENU 1
Clockwise from the bottom: starter platter containing Sesame Chicken Toast Triangles (above), Mini Spring Rolls (page 66) and Beef Satay (page 68), Toffee Apples (page 171), Shrimp Fried Rice (page 167), Cantonese Lemon Chicken (page 129), Stir-fry Beef with Green Peppers and Black Bean Sauce (page 105), and Traditional Sweet and Sour Sauce (page 86).

Facing page 65 THE FAVOURITE RESTAURANT MENU 2
Clockwise from the top: Lychees (page 172), Prawn Chow-mein (pages 78 and 83), Beef Chop Suey (pages 77 and 81), Egg Fried Rice (page 166), Chicken and Sweetcorn Soup (page 55), Sweet and Sour Pork (page 87), Hoisin Sauce (page 40), and Prawn Crackers (page 49).

SHANGHAI CRAB CLAWS

Makes 8 claws

This splendid highly decorative starter does require a little work but is well worth the effort, especially if you are entertaining. In this respect it is helpful to remember that they can be made well in advance then frozen or chilled and reheated in the deep-fryer when needed. Serve with one of the sweet and sour sauces on page 86 or Peking Dip Sauce (see page 53).

1 lb (450 g) raw prawns, thawed if frozen and peeled
2 cloves garlic, peeled and finely chopped
2 spring onions, finely chopped
1 teaspoon spicy salt
1 teaspoon cornflour, plus a little extra for dipping

8 crab claws
2 eggs, beaten
breadcrumbs for dipping

Garnish
finely shredded lettuce
mustard and cress
decoratively sliced red peppers

1. Place the prawns, garlic, spring onions, spicy salt and the teaspoon of cornflour in a food processor. Pulse gently until a coarse purée is obtained.

2. Carefully remove the shell from the crab claws to expose the meat, leaving just the tips of the claws to enable you to hold them firmly.

3. Divide the purée into eight.

4. Take one claw and cover the crab meat with the purée, leaving just the claw tip uncovered. Smooth and round the purée. Dip it in cornflour and set aside.

5. Repeat stage 4 with the remaining seven claws.

6. Heat the deep-fryer to 375°F/190°C (chip-frying temperature)

7. Dip the purée-covered end of one claw in beaten egg then dip it in breadcrumbs. Place it straight into the fryer.

8. Repeat stage 7 with the remaining claws.

9. After 10 minutes, remove the claws in the order you put them in and drain on absorbent kitchen paper.

10. Serve hot on a bed of shredded lettuce garnished with mustard and cress and pieces of red pepper.

MINI SPRING ROLLS

Makes 8 rolls

The recipe for full-sized spring rolls is on pages 100–103. They are about 4 inches (10 cm) long and are quite filling. These miniature spring rolls, however, are just 2 inches (5 cm) long and make elegant little canapés or starters.

Pastry
2 sheets spring roll pastry (see page
    100) or filo pastry, each 10 inches
    (25 cm) square
1 tablespoon cornflour

Filling
8 tablespoons of your chosen filling
    (see pages 100 and 102–3)

1. Cut each sheet of pastry into four.

2. Follow the rolling and filling instructions on page 101, using just 1 tablespoon of filling for each roll.

3. Heat the deep-fryer to 375°F/190°C (chip-frying temperature).

4. Place the spring rolls one by one into the fryer.

5. Cook for about 5–6 minutes until golden.

6. Remove from the fryer, shaking off any excess oil. Drain on absorbent kitchen paper for a minute or two. Serve hot.

Note: Cooked spring rolls can be frozen. To reheat from frozen follow the recipe above from stage 3.

MINI BARBECUE SPARE RIBS

Makes 16 ribs

This recipe is a variation of the main spare rib recipe on page 116, but here the ribs are miniature. An obliging butcher, given sufficient warning, may be able to obtain piglet ribs for you. Mini Spare Ribs make a very appealing starter or party nibble.

16 piglet ribs, total weight 1 lb   *spring onion tassels for garnish*
  (450 g)   *(see page 31)*
3 tablespoons hoisin sauce

1. Place the ribs in a dish, coat with the sauce, cover and leave to marinate in the fridge for a minimum of 3 hours and a maximum of 12 hours.

2. Heat the oven to 375°F/190°C/Gas 5.

3. Place the ribs on a wire rack standing in an oven tray.

4. Bake for 10–15 minutes, after which time they should be cooked through and crispy. If not, allow to cook for a little longer.

5. Transfer to a serving dish and garnish with spring onion tassels. Serve immediately.

BEEF OR CHICKEN SATAY

Makes 4 satay sticks

This is not strictly a Chinese dish; it hails from Indonesia. However it appears on the menu of many Chinese restaurants and does make a very good starter. It is especially tasty when given Chinese flavourings such as rice wine and soy sauce. Satay, by the way, means skewer and you will need four of these as specified below. Bamboo ones will need soaking in water for half an hour before use to prevent them from scorching during the cooking process. Otherwise use metal skewers.

four 8-inch (20-cm) bamboo skewers
1 lb (450 g) fillet steak
plum sauce, chilli sauce or hoisin
  sauce to serve

Marinade
2 tablespoons peanut butter
2 tablespoons Chinese yellow rice
  wine or dry sherry
1 tablespoon light soy sauce
1 teaspoon chilli and garlic sauce
½ teaspoon curry powder

1. Soak the skewers in water for half an hour.

2. Cut the steak into 1-inch (2.5 cm) squares about ¼ inch (6 mm) thick.

3. Using a meat mallet, pound the squares of meat until they measure about 1½ inches (3.75 cm) square by ⅙ inch (4 mm) thick.

4. Mix the marinade ingredients together in a bowl.

5. Immerse the meat in the marinade, cover and leave in the fridge for a minimum of 3 hours and a maximum of 24 hours.

6. Heat the grill to medium heat and place the rack at medium height.

7. Thread equal quantities of meat on to each of the skewers, leaving a little space between each piece of meat.

8. Place the skewers in the grill pan and cook for about 4–5 minutes, turning once.

9. Serve hot with plum, chilli or hoisin sauce for dipping.

THE CHINESE SALAD

Serves 4

There is no salad combination more delicious than that of raw beansprouts with mooli and Chinese leaves. I was once served this splendid salad in a halved pineapple, which would be an impressive way of serving it for a dinner party.

3 oz (75 g) mooli
2 oz (50 g) Chinese leaves
3 oz (75 g) carrot
3 oz (75 g) cucumber
½ red pepper
2 cloves garlic, peeled
3 or 4 pieces pickled ginger
3 oz (75 g) beansprouts
2 tablespoons finely chopped fresh
* coriander*
2 pineapples, to serve (optional)

Dressing
6 tablespoons cold vegetable stock
3 tablespoons Chinese white rice
* vinegar (or any type)*
2 tablespoons sesame oil
1 tablespoon sesame seed paste
* (tahini)*
1 tablespoon light soy sauce
1 teaspoon hoisin sauce
½ teaspoon spicy salt

1. Shred the mooli, Chinese leaves and carrot in 2-inch (5-cm) pieces.

2. Dice the cucumber and peppers into small pieces.

3. Finely chop the garlic and pickled ginger.

4. In a large bowl mix together all the vegetables and the coriander. Place in the fridge for up to an hour. Mix the dressing ingredients together and set aside.

5. Halve the pineapples lengthways, if using, and carefully scoop out the core and flesh. Use the flesh for another dish.

6. Ten minutes prior to serving, add the dressing to the vegetables then carefully put the salad into each pineapple half. Alternatively serve in salad bowls.

THE CHRYSANTHEMUM FIRE POT

Also known as Mongolian hot pot or steamboat, this is a performance dish or entertaining spectacular. The dish was originally introduced to China when the savage Mongol hordes broke through the Chinese wall and ruled China in the thirteenth century. The Mongolian hot pot was one legacy the invaders left. The fragrant edible chrysanthemum was an addition introduced by the chefs of Canton.

The dish makes a superlative starter. Raw ingredients are prepared for cooking and placed decoratively on serving plates. You will need a special table-top cooking stove. There are two versions. One has a central chimney akin to the Mongol design, the other does not. Both have lids to cover the stock. Traditionally both were charcoal fired, now they are meths or even gas operated. It is customary to control the heat of the charcoal fire by placing a serving bowl on top to damp down and cool the flame if it gets too hot. These are obtainable from Chinese or Japanese specialist shops. A fondue pot is an acceptable substitute. The stove is placed in the centre of the table. The diners select the item they want to eat, then place it with chopsticks into the saucepan which contains simmering stock. After a short time the item is withdrawn, dunked in the dip(s) and eaten piping hot. It is a fun dish and plenty of time should be allowed to get through it. It encourages chatter and laughter all of which makes it excellent for entertaining.

The chrysanthemum element is traditional, very attractive visually and gives the dish its name. The petals are floated in the hot stock and can be eaten. They are an optional ingredient if you can't get them. Chinese poets were extolling the edible virtues of this flower thousands of years ago. Apothecaries encouraged its use in many forms, medicinally, and chrysanthemum tea is still taken to this day.

Stock
sufficient clear chicken, vegetable or
   vintage master stock to fulfil stage
   1 and have some reserve
2–3 chrysanthemums, optional

Ingredients
raw king prawns, peeled but with tails
   on
small raw prawns, peeled
chicken breast
beef and/or pork fillet
cooked egg noodles or rice vermicelli
pak-choi (Chinese cabbage)
red and green peppers
carrots
Chinese radish
lotus root

Dips
hoisin sauce
plum sauce
chilli sauce
sesame paste
Pekinese dip sauce
chilli oil

Accompaniments
pickled ginger
vinegared chillies
pickled vegetables

1. Fill the cooking pot about two-thirds full with the stock and place it on the table.

2. Prepare the ingredients. Choose at least six items. As a starter for four you will need about 12 oz (350 g) total weight of items. Keep the prawns whole but remove the vein from the king prawns by cutting lightly down the back. Wash and dry them. Slice the chicken and/or meats. Coarsely shred the pak-choi. Cut the peppers into diamond shapes. Cut the carrots and Chinese radish into strips. Slice the lotus root across.

3. Place your selection on serving plates and keep chilled until you need it. Place the dips in small serving bowls and the accompaniments in slightly larger bowls.

4. Light the cooking pot heat source shortly before you sit down at table so that the stock will be simmering by the time you are ready to begin.

5. Just prior to serving pluck the petals from the chrysanthemums and float them in the hot stock.

6. Each diner picks up an item, say a piece of chicken, with chopsticks. The chicken is placed in the simmering stock. When the piece is cooked the diner removes it from the stock and dips into a dip or dips of their choice. Accompany with pickled ginger, vinegared chillies and pickled vegetables. The noodles can be eaten in the same way, or they can be served with the stock at the end of the meal, by which time it will have reduced to a tasty broth.

THE CHICKEN AND THE EGG

Serves 4

This astonishingly attractive starter is easier to make than it looks. It is made in three layers. The bottom is thinly sliced overlapped chicken breasts. Over this is spread finely-ground chicken mixed with either prawns or meat. This is steamed, then it is covered with egg white and it is steamed again to give the top a pure white surface. The final embellishment of red pepper and chives transforms the dish into a truly elegant canapé or starter. The photo opposite page 161 says it all. It does not solve the riddle of which came first.

9 oz (275 g) raw chicken breast fillets
2 oz (50 g) ham, fat removed
6 oz (175 g) small raw prawns, peeled
1 teaspoon spicy salt
1 tablespoon cornflour
4 egg whites

Garnish
slices of red pepper
chives

1. Line a round steamer basket of about 8 inches (20 cm) diameter with kitchen foil.

2. Set aside one third of the chicken breast fillets. Slice each of the remaining fillets through the middle into two thin slices. Beat the slices until they are as thin as a slice of ham.

3. Line the foil with the chicken slices. There will be enough slices to overlap and to double line the basket.

4. Put the reserved chicken breast fillets into a food processor or hand mincer along with the ham, prawns, salt and cornflour.

5. Pulse or mince into a coarse paste. Spread this on to the chicken slices.

6. Put the lid on the basket, place over boiling water and steam for about 15 minutes.

7. Beat the egg whites but do not allow them to become frothy.

8. At the end of stage 6 spread the beaten egg white over the cooked paste.

9. Steam for a further 5 minutes. Remove the basket from the steamer and allow to cool completely.

10. Remove from the foil and cut into wedges like a cake. Trim the round edges by cutting straight across to form triangles.

11. Decorate with the slices of pepper and the chives.

MARBLED EGGS or TEA EGGS

Makes 4 eggs

Often confused with hundred year eggs (see glossary), these are hard-boiled eggs which have a really attractive marbled look to them. The traditional colouring is tea, but modern restaurateurs use red, blue, green or yellow food colouring to achieve a more colourful effect. Serve cold as a garnish or as a part of a starter selection.

1 pint (600 ml) water
4 eggs

4 teabags or 1 teaspoon appropriate
food colouring

1. Boil the water in a pan.

2. Prick the blunt end of each egg with a pin to prevent premature cracking. Place the eggs into the boiling water.

3. Reduce the heat and simmer for about 8 minutes.

4. Remove the eggs from the water. Add the teabags or food colouring to the water.

5. Gently tap the eggs with the back of a knife to create a 'crazy-paving' effect all over them, but do not remove any shell.

6. Place the eggs back into the simmering water, which is now coloured, and simmer for 4 more minutes. Turn off the heat and set aside for 12–24 hours.

7. After this time drain them and remove the shells to reveal your prettily marbled eggs.

PHOENIX COLD MEAT PLATTER

Chinese cooking stems from antiquity and is steeped in tradition. The names of dishes, their general presentation and the combination of ingredients have varied little over centuries. The phoenix is a Chinese symbol of excellence and continuity and is often represented in food terms. This is one such dish. Here it is very graphic, being a picturesque mosaic of cold meats and vegetables. It takes a long time to lay out so is rarely seen in restaurants. It is fun to do, however, and is a great talking piece for entertaining.

Use any sliced cooked meat or vegetables to create your masterpiece – your imagination is your limit.

cooked chicken breast, sliced
roast beef or cha-siu, sliced
ham, sliced
cooked lamb's liver, sliced
cooked prawns, peeled
cucumber
boiled quail's eggs

black Chinese mushrooms
maraschino cherries
carrot
red and green pepper
red and green chilli
a few peas

1. Examine the illustration below. Choose a flat round plate or dish about 10 inches (25 cm) in diameter.

2. Cut the chicken to make the head, neck and breast. Build these up in layers with small decoratively cut pieces.

3. Cut the beef to create the wing feathers and the ham to make the tail feathers.

4. Build up colour and texture with contrasting shapes and pieces to your liking.

5. Use the remaining ingredients to obtain maximum effect.

6. Your phoenix can be largely prepared well in advance, and kept covered in the fridge until you need it. Simply finish it off with any vegetables (which will 'weep' if put in too soon) just prior to serving.

CHAPTER 5

✠

CHINESE RESTAURANT FAVOURITES

In this chapter I have grouped together the most popular Chinese restaurant dishes. These are Chop Suey, Chow-mein (soft noodles), Chinese Curry, Foo Yung (omelette), sweet and sour dishes, wontons, Spring Rolls and stir-fry sliced meat dishes.

These are the dishes which appear on the standard Cantonese Chinese restaurant menu all over the world. To the uninitiated the standard menu seems to be long and complicated, with a choice often exceeding 100 dishes. Ordering by numbers is the norm in such establishments. A meal for four might consist of one each of five items. The standard menu actually appears more complicated than it is because there are several variations for each dish. Chop Suey, for example, has seven popular variations – King Prawn Chop Suey, Beef Chop Suey, Chicken, Pork, Mixed Vegetable and Special Chop Suey (the latter being a combination of the previous ingredients). Similarly the other eight dishes given in this chapter each have their own variations and from these ten main dishes we can produce no less than 65 variations.

The restaurants can work the apparent miracle of producing any of their 100-plus dishes within a few minutes of the customer ordering them, by the application of a simple technique. They have principal ingredients such as prawns, beef, chicken, duck, pork and vegetables ready cut and chilled, and even in some cases pre-cooked. Sauces are also prepared in advance and chilled. Rice and noodles are pre-cooked and kept warm. It is then a relatively simple matter of mixing principal ingredients with the required sauce, stir-frying and serving.

CHOP SUEY

Serves 4

No other words are more associated with Chinese food than Chop Suey. Yet, amazingly, the words themselves do not occur anywhere in China. The name appears to have originated at the turn of the century in the restaurants of the world's first Chinatown in San Francisco. It means chopped mixed food. Chop Suey is traditionally served with rice or noodles.

There are many types of Chop Suey, ranging from beef or pork to vegetable or prawn. They all start out as the same basic recipe to which is added the appropriate principal ingredient. Select a principal ingredient from those listed on pages 81–4 and add to the basic Chop Suey recipe below at stage 3.

2 tablespoons light vegetable oil
1 clove garlic, peeled and finely
    chopped
1 inch (2.5 cm) cube fresh ginger,
    peeled and finely chopped
6 spring onions, thinly sliced
2 oz (50 g) mangetout
$\frac{1}{4}$ pint (150 ml) chicken or vegetable
    stock, or water
1 lb (450 g) prepared principal
    ingredient(s) (see pages 81–4)

2 oz (50 g) beansprouts
1 oz (25 g) dried black Chinese
    mushrooms, reconstituted
    (see page 146)
1 oz (25 g) water chestnuts
1 oz (25 g) canned bamboo shoots
    (optional)
1 tablespoon potato flour (optional)
1 tablespoon Chinese yellow rice wine
    or dry sherry
2 teaspoons light soy sauce

1. Heat the oil in a wok until it simmers. Throw in the garlic, ginger and spring onions and stir-fry briskly for 30 seconds.

2. Add the mangetout and continue stir-frying for a further 30 seconds.

3. Add the stock or water and bring to the simmer. Add your chosen main ingredient, along with the beansprouts, Chinese mushrooms, water chestnuts and the optional bamboo shoots. Stir-fry for a couple of minutes.

4. Sprinkle in the optional potato flour to thicken the dish a little, if you wish, then add the wine and soy sauce. Briskly stir-fry until the liquid simmers. It is then ready to serve.

CHOW-MEIN

— · —

Serves 4

Chow-mein translates as stir-fried noodles. The argument has raged for centuries as to who invented noodles – was it the Italians with their pasta or was it the Chinese? Their trading connections predate written history, so who knows? The fact is that noodles have always been a major part of the Chinese culinary heritage.

As with Chop Suey, I give one basic Chow-mein recipe to which is added a choice of principal ingredients: beef, chicken, pork, king prawn, prawn, vegetable or a 'special' (see pages 81–4).

8 oz (225 g) egg noodles
2 tablespoons light vegetable oil
1–2 cloves garlic, peeled and finely
  chopped
1 inch (2.5 cm) cube fresh ginger,
  peeled and finely chopped
6 spring onions, sliced
3 fl oz (75 ml) chicken or vegetable
  stock, or water
1 lb (450 g) prepared principal
  ingredient(s) (see pages 81–4)

4 Chinese mushrooms, reconstituted
  (see page 146)
1 oz (25 g) canned bamboo shoots,
  sliced (optional)
1 oz (25 g) green pepper, cut into
  small dice
1 tablespoon Chinese yellow rice wine
  or dry sherry
2 teaspoons light soy sauce
1 tablespoon potato flour

1. Soft boil the noodles as described on page 159. Drain and set aside, keeping warm. Alternatively they can be reheated prior to stage 4 below.

2. Heat the oil in a wok until it starts to simmer. Throw in the garlic, ginger and spring onions and stir-fry briskly for 30 seconds.

3. Add the stock and when it simmers add your chosen principal ingredient and the mushrooms, optional bamboo shoots and green pepper. Stir-fry for a couple of minutes.

4. Add the wine or sherry and soy sauce and, if you like a thicker sauce, the optional potato flour. Stir-fry briskly until simmering, then add the noodles, mixing them in carefully. The chow-mein is now ready to serve.

CHINESE CURRY

Serves 4

One is unlikely to find curry in China, but Chinese restaurants around the world have developed their own style of curry. It is quite different from that of India, being sweetish and mild. This recipe uses fruit squash to enhance the flavour.

Again I give the basic recipe to which is added one or a combination of principal ingredients (see pages 81–4).

1 tablespoon mild curry powder or
  bottled curry paste
1 teaspoon Chinese five-spice powder
1 tablespoon cornflour
water
3 tablespoons vegetable oil
4 oz (110 g) onion, peeled and finely
  chopped

1 lb (450 g) prepared principal
  ingredient(s) (see pages 81–4)
1 teaspoon orange squash concentrate
1 teaspoon granulated sugar
1 tablespoon tomato ketchup
salt to taste

1. Mix the curry powder or paste and five-spice powder together with a little water, if necessary, to make a stiffish paste. Leave it to stand for a few minutes.

2. Meanwhile mix the cornflour with $1–1\frac{1}{2}$ tablespoons water to make a smooth runny paste the consistency of milk.

3. Warm the cornflour paste in a saucepan, stirring continuously to prevent it going lumpy. When it starts to thicken, add a little more water. Keep stirring. When it starts to thicken again add a little more water. Repeat this process until it will not thicken further. You are aiming for a thickish sauce. Put it aside, keeping it warm.

4. Heat the oil in a wok. Stir-fry the onion for a couple of minutes. Add the curry paste and stir-fry for a further minute.

5. Add the principal ingredient of your choice and stir-fry briskly for a couple of minutes.

6. Add the warm cornflour sauce, orange squash concentrate, sugar and tomato ketchup. Mix together thoroughly then add salt to taste and serve.

Note: This dish does not freeze well – it goes acidic.

FOO YUNG (OMELETTE)

Serves 4

As with many of the dishes in this chapter, omelettes are not a regular feature in authentic Chinese cuisine. At the Chinese restaurant, however, they are popular and very tasty, either on their own as a light meal or as an accompaniment.

As with previous recipes in this chapter, restaurants add a variety of principal ingredients to the omelette. Choose from those listed on pages 81–4.

1 tablespoon soy or sunflower oil
1 clove garlic, peeled and finely
  chopped
4 spring onions with leaves, sliced
1 tablespoon red pepper, cut into small
  dice

$\frac{1}{2}$ quantity prepared principal
  ingredient (see pages 81–4)
salt to taste
4 eggs
$\frac{1}{2}$ tablespoon butter

1. To make the filling heat the oil in a wok and stir-fry the garlic, spring onion and pepper for 2 minutes. Add the principal ingredient of your choice and stir-fry until it is quite hot. Add salt to taste. Remove from the wok and keep warm.

2. During stage 1, beat the eggs with a wire whisk.

3. Heat the butter in a large flat frying pan.

4. Pour the whisked egg into the pan and cook on medium heat until it firms up. Carefully turn over then spread with filling. Continue cooking until the egg is firm.

5. Fold or roll the omelette over, cut into quarters or strips and serve hot.

Preparation of principal ingredients for:
Chop Suey, Chow-mein, Chinese Curry and *Foo Yung*

To the basic recipes for Chop Suey, Chow-mein and Chinese Curry and Foo Yung the restaurants add a further principal ingredient, or combination of ingredients. Here are the seven most popular variants: beef, chicken, pork, king prawn, prawn, mixed vegetable and a 'special'.

BEEF

1 lb (450 g) fillet steak or top side of beef

custard powder for dipping
2 tablespoons light vegetable oil

1. Cut the beef across the grain into strips about 2 inches (5 cm) long, 1 inch (2.5 cm) wide and $\frac{1}{8}$ inch (3 mm) thick.

2. Dip the strips into the custard powder.

3. Heat the oil in a wok or frying pan.

4. Add the beef strips to the wok piece by piece rather than all at once (this maintains a high temperature), stirring all the time.

5. Once the meat is cooked right through (after about 5 minutes), remove from the wok and keep warm while you prepare the basic Chop Suey, Chow-mein, Chinese Curry or Foo Yung recipe.

CHICKEN

— . —

1 lb (450 g) skinless chicken breast
   fillet

cornflour for dipping
2 tablespoons light vegetable oil

1. Cut the chicken breast into strips about 2 inches (5 cm) long, $\frac{1}{2}$ inch (1.25 cm) wide and $\frac{1}{4}$ inch (6 mm) thick.

2. Dip the strips into the cornflour.

3. Heat the oil in a wok or frying pan.

4. Add the chicken strips to the wok piece by piece rather than all at once (this maintains a high temperature), stirring all the time.

5. Once the chicken is cooked right through (after about 4 minutes) remove from the wok and keep warm while you prepare the basic Chop Suey, Chow-mein, Chinese Curry or Foo Yung recipe.

PORK

— . —

1 lb (450 g) lean pork
cornflour for dipping
2 tablespoons light vegetable oil

1. Remove all unwanted matter from the pork and dice it into small cubes about $\frac{3}{4}$ inch (2 cm) square.

2. Dip the cubes into the cornflour.

3. Heat the oil in a wok or frying pan.

4. Add the pork cubes piece by piece rather than all at once (this maintains a high temperature), stirring all the time.

5. Once the pork is cooked right through (after about 6 minutes) remove from the wok and keep warm while you prepare the basic Chop Suey, Chow-mein, Chinese Curry or Foo Yung recipe.

KING PRAWN
—— . ——

1 lb (450 g) king prawns, weighed
after stage 1
2 tablespoons light vegetable oil

1. Remove the shells, heads and tails from the prawns. Carefully slit down the back of each with the point of a knife and remove the vein. Wash and dry them.

2. Heat the oil in a wok or frying pan.

3. Add the king prawns one at a time rather than all at once (this maintains a high temperature), stirring all the time.

4. Once the king prawns are cooked right through (after about 4–6 minutes depending on their size) remove from the wok but keep warm while you prepare the basic Chop Suey, Chow-mein, Chinese Curry or Foo Yung recipe.

PRAWN
—— . ——

1 lb (450 g) raw prawns, thawed and *2 tablespoons light vegetable oil*
drained if frozen, and weighed after
stage 1

1. Remove the shells, heads and tails from the prawns. If necessary remove the vein (see stage 1 of the previous recipe). Wash and dry them.

2. Heat the oil in a wok or frying pan.

3. Add the prawns a few at a time rather than all at once (this maintains a high temperature), stirring all the time.

4. Once the prawns are cooked right through (after about 5 minutes), remove from the wok but keep warm while you prepare the basic Chop Suey, Chow-mein, Chinese Curry or Foo Yung recipe.

MIXED VEGETABLES
— · —

6 oz (175 g) broccoli, cut into tiny
  florets
6 oz (175 g) carrot, cut into strips

4 oz (110 g) pak-choi (Chinese
  cabbage) cut into short thin strips

1. Bring a large saucepan of water to the boil.

2. Blanch the broccoli florets for 4 minutes and the carrot strips for 2 or 3 minutes.

3. Drain and keep warm while you prepare the basic Chop Suey, Chow-mein, Chinese Curry or Foo Yung recipe. (The pak-choi does not require blanching.)

SPECIAL
— · —

Many restaurants combine a number of ingredients such as beef, prawns and vegetable to make their own special variation. Select a combination of principal ingredients and prepare as described in the previous recipes, to make your own personalised version of Chop Suey, Chow-mein, Chinese Curry or Foo Yung. You will need about 1 lb (450 g) of raw principal ingredients in total.

SWEET AND SOUR DISHES

Undoubtedly one of China's culinary masterpieces is the superb combination of battered items immersed in a sweet and sour sauce. This is a very ancient Chinese dish that originated in the Cantonese area in South China.

The filling – which can be anything from pork to prawn or even tofu (see pages 87 and 89–90) – is marinated in soy sauce, hoisin sauce and Chinese wine before being fried in batter and coated in the famous sauce. The bulk of the method can be prepared in advance, leaving just the frying to be done on the night.

Prepare the batter and the sweet and sour sauce first, then follow the main recipe on page 87.

The batter

There are two types of batter used for sweet and sour dishes. In the traditional recipe the flour and egg batter coats the main ingredient (whether meat, fish or vegetable) and it is stir-fried. The restaurant version, which contains no egg, deep-fries it instead and the result is a light puffy batter. Each way has its own merits, so I give both recipes here. Cooking instructions are on pages 87 and 88.

TRADITIONAL BATTER

5 oz (150 g) cornflour
1 egg
water to mix

Mix the cornflour and egg together then add sufficient water to make a stiffish but pourable batter paste.

PUFFY BATTER

1 oz (25 g) cornflour
7 oz (200 g) plain white flour
½ teaspoon baking powder
⅓ teaspoon salt

⅓ teaspoon granulated sugar
1 tablespoon vegetable oil
12 fl oz (350 ml) water

1. Mix all the dry ingredients together.

2. Add all the oil, then add the water little by little, mixing between each addition to make a smooth paste of pouring consistency. Let it stand for about 20 minutes before using.

The sauce

There are as many recipes for sweet and sour sauce as there are Chinese cooks. Here are just two.

TRADITIONAL SWEET AND SOUR SAUCE
— · —

1 tablespoon cornflour
4 fl oz (100 ml) distilled malt vinegar
4 oz (110 g) granulated sugar
2 tablespoons light soy sauce
2 tablespoons tomato ketchup

2 tablespoons pineapple juice
   (optional)
2 tablespoons Chinese yellow rice
   wine or sweet sherry (optional)

1. Mix the cornflour with enough of the vinegar to make a thin paste. Set aside.

2. Place the remaining vinegar, the sugar, soy sauce, ketchup and pineapple juice in a pan and bring to the simmer.

3. Remove from the heat and stir in the cornflour paste.

4. Return the pan to the heat and stir continuously until it stops thickening. Add the rice wine at this stage and thin with a little water if necessary.

5. Serve hot or allow to cool then pour into bottles to use when required.

FRUITY SWEET AND SOUR SAUCE
— · —

1 tangerine or satsuma, peel and pith
   removed
$\frac{1}{3}$ oz (10 g) carrot, finely shredded

$\frac{1}{3}$ oz (10 g) pickled ginger, finely
   shredded

Add the above ingredients to the Traditional Sweet and Sour Sauce recipe at stage 2 and simmer the sauce for about 5 minutes. Proceed with the rest of the method.

SWEET AND SOUR PORK

Serves 4

Once you have prepared the batter and the sweet and sour sauce you can procede with this, the main recipe. Here I use pork as the filling, but for variations see pages 88–90

12 oz (350 g) boned and trimmed lean
  leg of pork
vegetable oil as necessary
1 quantity either Traditional or Puffy
  batter
1 quantity either Traditional or
  Fruity sweet and sour sauce

Marinade
2 tablespoons dark soy sauce
1 tablespoon hoisin sauce
1 tablespoon Chinese yellow rice wine
  or sweet sherry

1. Cut the pork into $\frac{3}{4}$ inch (2 cm) cubes.

2. To make the marinade, mix the soy sauce, hoisin sauce and wine in a bowl large enough to hold the pork.

3. Add the pork, cover and leave in the fridge for at least 1 hour or, better still, overnight (but for a maximum of 24 hours).

4. Drain the meat and dry it by placing it on absorbent kitchen paper.

5. Heat a little oil in a wok or frying pan and stir-fry the pork for 5–6 minutes.

6. Remove from the heat, strain and allow to go cold.

7. Follow the method of frying for Traditional Batter or Puffy Batter as appropriate (see below and page 88).

TRADITIONAL BATTER METHOD OF FRYING

1. Heat 4 tablespoons oil in a wok.

2. Dip the pork into the batter and place it piece by piece rather than all at once into the wok (this maintains a high temperature). Stir-fry for about 4 minutes, turning as necessary. You may need to cook the pork in two batches.

3. Remove the cooked meat from the wok and drain on kitchen paper.

4. Meanwhile heat the sweet and sour sauce. Place the hot battered meat in a bowl and pour over the sauce. Serve at once.

PUFFY BATTER METHOD OF FRYING

1. Heat the deep-fryer to 375°F/190°C (chip-frying temperature).

2. Dip one piece of the pork into the batter and place it at once into the fryer. Repeat with more pieces of pork until a layer is floating in the fryer (this should use up about half the pork).

3. Fry them for about 10 minutes, turning as necessary.

4. Remove from the fryer, shaking off excess oil, drain on absorbent kitchen paper then keep warm while you batter and fry the second batch of meat.

5. Meanwhile heat the sweet and sour sauce. Place the battered pork balls into a serving bowl. Pour the sauce over them and serve at once.

The filling variations

The three most common restaurant fillings for sweet and sour dishes are pork, chicken and king prawn. Other interesting variations are fish, tofu and cauliflower. The same general method is used for all: the filling is marinated before being coated in batter and fried. All the fillings except fish and tofu have to be pre-cooked before being coated and fried in batter. Follow the general method for Sweet and Sour Pork (see page 87), substituting your chosen filling for the pork.

All fillings serve 4.

SWEET AND SOUR CHICKEN

Follow the method for Sweet and Sour Pork, substituting 12 oz (350 g) skinless boned chicken meat for the pork.

SWEET AND SOUR KING PRAWN

Follow the method for Sweet and Sour Pork, substituting 24 shelled and de-veined king prawns for the pork.

SWEET AND SOUR FISH

12 oz (350 g) cod steak
remaining ingredients as for Sweet
and Sour Pork (see page 87)

1. Cut the steak(s) into $\frac{3}{4}$ inch (2 cm) pieces.

2. Follow stages 2 and 3 of the method for Sweet and Sour Pork, immersing the pieces in the marinade for 30 minutes. Drain the fish and dry it by placing it on absorbent kitchen paper.

3. Follow the frying method for Traditional or Puffy batter, allowing less time cooking in the wok or deep-fryer.

SWEET AND SOUR TOFU

12 oz (350 g) tofu block
remaining ingredients as for Sweet
and Sour Pork (see page 87)

1. Cut the tofu into $\frac{1}{2}$ inch (1.25 cm) pieces.

2. Follow stages 2 and 3 of the method for Sweet and Sour Pork, immersing the pieces in the marinade for 1 hour. Drain the tofu and dry it by placing it on absorbent kitchen paper.

3. Omit stages 5 and 6 (the pre-cooking) and follow the frying method for Traditional or Puffy batter, as appropriate.

SWEET AND SOUR CAULIFLOWER

*12 oz (350 g) cauliflower cut into
small florets*

*remaining ingredients as for Sweet
and Sour Pork (see page 87)*

1. Blanch the cauliflower in boiling water for 2–3 minutes. Drain and cool.

2. Follow stages 2 and 3 of the method for Sweet and Sour Pork, immersing the florets in the marinade for a couple of hours. Drain and dry them by placing them on absorbent kitchen paper.

3. Omit stages 5 and 6 and follow the frying method for Traditional or Puffy batter, as appropriate.

WONTONS

Makes 24–30

There appears to be slight confusion about dim sum and wontons. They appear on many a restaurant menu as if they are one and the same thing. They are not. Dim sum literally means 'heart's delight', and refers to any tiny, attractive bite-sized snacks. In China they are served at any time of day in their own right or as starters. Tea shops in China specialise exclusively in dim sum, serving them from breakfast to night time with the ubiquitous bowls of China tea.

Dim sum can include a number of different types of snack other than pastry items. The best known dim sum are those made with very thin pastry and known as wontons. The pastry was developed in the seventh century in Peking and is made from wheat flour and egg. The filling can be savoury or sweet and wontons can be steamed, stir-fried, baked or deep-fried. They are made in a variety of traditional shapes (see pages 94–6) but they are always diminutive.

Wonton wrappers (also known as sheets or skins) are extremely thinly rolled sheets of dough made from wheat flour and egg. The normal size of each sheet is around 3 inches (7.5 cm) square. Specialist bakers make this pastry and it takes years of training to produce translucently thin pastry of even thickness. For this reason it is convenient to buy the wrappers ready made. They are available at specialist shops, frozen, in packets of 24 or 30. If you cannot obtain them spring roll or filo pastry are perfectly acceptable alternatives. Wonton wrappers can be made at home quite easily – the only difficulty is rolling the dough out to tracing-paper thinness.

Whether home-made or bought always keep wonton wrappers covered with a clean damp tea towel until required for use to prevent them going brittle.

The quantities given here make about 24 wonton wrappers, depending on the thinness of your rolling

Wonton wrappers
8 oz (225 g) strong white flour plus
  extra for dusting
1 egg
water to mix
1 tablespoon cornflour

Filling
1 quantity of your chosen filling (see
page 93) or a selection of fillings

Wonton wrappers

1. Place the flour in a large bowl and mix in the egg.

2. Add sufficient water to make a stiffish dough, kneading until it becomes well mixed and smooth. Set aside for 20–30 minutes.

3. Mix the cornflour with sufficient water to make a paste. Set aside to use later when you are filling and shaping the Wontons in stage 7.

4. Dust the work surface with flour. Knead the dough once more, then halve it.

5. Knead one half into an approximate square then roll it out as thin as you can get it. Do this fast and don't worry if it is uneven. Cut into squares of about 3 inches (7.5 cm). Dust each square with flour and stack one on top of the other. Cover with a clean damp cloth. This must all be done quickly to prevent the wrappers going brittle.

6. Gather up any spare off-cuts and knead them into the other half of the dough. Repeat stage 5 until all the dough is rolled, cut and stacked. Use fairly soon or freeze.

Filling and shaping

7. Follow the filling, folding and pasting techniques for your chosen wonton shapes (see pages 94–6).

Cooking

8. Wontons can be steamed, deep-fried, stir-fried or baked. Follow the instructions on pages 97–9.

Wonton fillings

There are as many wonton fillings as there are people to think them up. The most important factor is that the ingredients must be chopped small to make the entire item dainty. Here I give a number of typical savoury fillings and on page 174 I give a sweet filling.

Simply purée all the ingredients together in a food processor or hand mincer to make a coarse purée. Divide the mixture into six. Each division will give 6 teaspoons of filling – enough to fill 6 wontons (36 in total). Freeze any leftover filling for future use.

PORK AND PRAWN

3 oz (75 g) pork, finely minced
3 oz (75 g) prawns, fresh or frozen, thawed, and peeled

2 cloves garlic, peeled and finely chopped
1 spring onion, finely chopped

CHICKEN AND HAM

3 oz (75 g) chicken, finely minced
3 oz (75 g) ham, finely minced
1 spring onion, finely chopped

1 clove garlic, peeled and finely chopped

FISH AND CRAB

3 oz (75 g) white fish, such as haddock or cod

3 oz (75 g) white crab meat
1 spring onion, finely chopped

BEEF AND BEANSPROUTS

3 oz (75 g) beef, finely minced
1 oz (25 g) beansprouts, chopped
1 spring onion, finely chopped

1 clove garlic, peeled and finely chopped

GREEN VEGETABLES

2 oz (50 g) cabbage, shredded
1 clove garlic, peeled and finely chopped

1 spring onion, finely chopped
$\frac{1}{2}$ teaspoon hoisin sauce

Wonton shapes

Wonton wrappers are used with fillings to create a wide range of shapes. Here are the most common ones:

WONTON TUBE (or Mini Spring Roll see page 66)

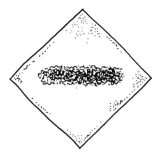

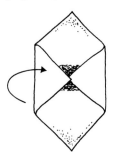

1. place filling in centre of a wonton sheet

2. fold in outside flaps

3. fold in other flaps

4. roll up tightly, and seal with cornflour paste

WONTON HALF MOON

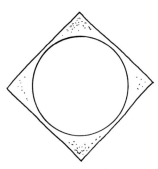

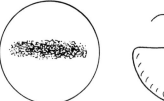

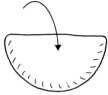

1. cut a circle of about 3 inches (7.5 cm) diameter from a wonton wrapper

2. put some filling in the centre and paste the edges with cornflour paste

3. fold over and press the curved sides together

WONTON DUMPLING (CHIAO TSU) or TREASURE BAGS

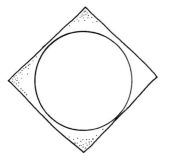 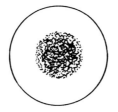

1. cut a circle of about 3 ins (7.5 cm) diameter from a wonton wrapper

2. put some filling in the centre

3. gather the edges together to form it into a sphere

4. squeeze it shut (side view)

WONTON CIRCLE

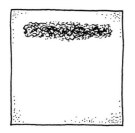 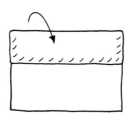 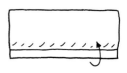

1. put some filling near the top of a wonton wrapper

2. fold over and press the edges together

3. fold over again and paste the seams down with cornflour paste

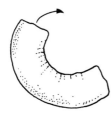 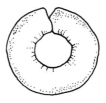

4. gently pull the pastry round

5. the wonton should end up in an approximate circle

WONTON CRACKER

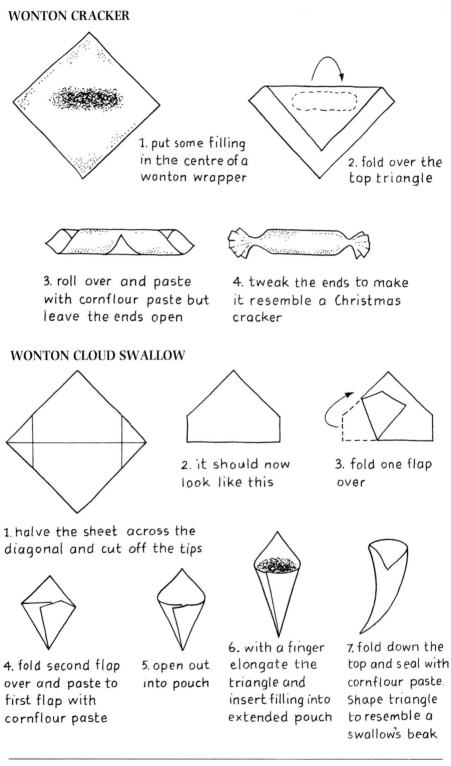

1. put some filling in the centre of a wonton wrapper

2. fold over the top triangle

3. roll over and paste with cornflour paste but leave the ends open

4. tweak the ends to make it resemble a Christmas cracker

WONTON CLOUD SWALLOW

2. it should now look like this

3. fold one flap over

1. halve the sheet across the diagonal and cut off the tips

4. fold second flap over and paste to first flap with cornflour paste

5. open out into pouch

6. with a finger elongate the triangle and insert filling into extended pouch

7. fold down the top and seal with cornflour paste. Shape triangle to resemble a swallow's beak

Wonton cooking

The most common method of cooking Wontons in China is by steaming, but they can also be deep-fried, stir-fried or baked.

STEAMING

Steaming in a wok is an important method of Chinese cooking. The technique is the same whatever you are steaming, only the size of basket required and the cooking time will vary.

A wok is partly filled with water which is then brought to the boil. A steamer rack is inserted which provides a base clear of the boiling water. The items to be steamed are placed into purpose designed bamboo steamers. These are available in a variety of sizes (see page 20).

They can be used singly or can be stacked one upon the other to a maximum of three or four baskets. The one on top has a bamboo lid placed on it. The basket or stack of baskets is then placed on the rack in the wok.

These steamers are relatively inexpensive and are well worth investing in. I prefer to use a saucepan rather than a wok to boil the water in as it takes up less space, and so I have obtained bamboo steamers that fit tightly into the top of my saucepans. This also means I can stack the baskets higher.

1. Half fill a saucepan with water and bring to the boil. If using a wok, place the steamer rack in the bottom and fill with water to within 1 inch (2.5 cm) of the top of the rack. Bring to the boil.

2. Whilst this is underway, line the bamboo baskets with some thin lettuce leaves. This prevents the pastries from sticking to the bamboo. Some restaurants oil the bamboo instead but I find that a layer of lettuce is more reliable.

3. Place the wontons into the baskets allowing a little space between them.

4. Place the basket(s) over the saucepan and put the bamboo lid on the top one. If using a wok, place the baskets on the stand and place the lid on the wok.

5. Reduce the heat to simmer. Leave to steam for about 10–15 minutes, checking throughout that there is sufficient water in the pan.

Facing page 96 SEA-TIME MENU
Clockwise from the top: Shanghai Crab Claws (page 65), Sesame Prawn Toasts (page 64), Five Willow Fish (page 143), Crispy Deep-fried Seaweed (page 50), Shark's Fin Soup (page 62), Oyster Black Beans (page 138), and Sea-spicy Noodle Balls (page 164).

Opposite SZECHWAN HOT AND SPICY MENU
From the top: Hot Spicy Chicken (page 127), Hot and Sour Soup (page 56), Szechwan Chilli Sauce (page 42), Szechwan Chilli Prawns (page 136), Vinegared Chillies (page 46), Pe-tsai with Ginger and Nuts (page 149), and Szechwan Duck (page 123).

DEEP-FRYING

All Wontons can be deep-fried as an alternative to steaming. Many people actually prefer the crispiness this achieves. You can use an electric deep-fryer or a wok for deep-frying. With the latter extreme care is required to avoid accidents.

1. If using an electric deep-fryer, heat it to 375°F/190°C (chip-frying temperature). If using a wok, half fill it with oil. Bring the oil to a temperature where a test piece of wonton wrapper sizzles and floats more or less at once when dropped in.

2. Put the Wontons into the hot oil one by one until there are enough in the pan to allow free movement but not too many to create congestion and the resultant drop in temperature.

3. Deep-fry until the Wontons are golden (6–10 minutes depending on the size). Stir once or twice to ensure they cook on all sides.

4. When cooked to your satisfaction remove from the oil and place on absorbent kitchen paper. After a couple of minutes they will be at their crispiest. Serve as hot as possible. They can be cooled and re-heated when required, but fresh is best. They can also be frozen.

STIR-FRYING

Wontons can indeed be stir-fried. They need constant and careful movement to ensure they cook thoroughly. They do not cook quite as evenly and crisply as when deep-fried, but the method is acceptable if you don't wish to set up the deep-fryer.

1. Pour oil into the wok to a minimum depth of 1 inch (2.5 cm).

2. Place one Wonton into the oil, moving it about until it stops sticking (about 10–25 seconds). Add the next, repeating the operation until the wok is full but not cluttered.

3. Stir-fry very carefully until they are as evenly cooked as you can get them. Repeat with the remaining wontons.

BAKING

The final method of cooking Wontons is by baking them in the oven. This produces crisp results without the calorific effects of frying, and is consequently favoured by some people.

1. Heat the oven to 375°C/190°F/Gas 5.

2. Select a suitable sized oven tray and line it with kitchen foil.

3. Place the Wontons on the foil, allowing a little space between each one.

4. Bake for 8–12 minutes (depending on the size of the Wontons) or until cooked to your liking.

SPRING OR PANCAKE ROLLS

Makes 30

These well known crispy cylinders of pastry, packed with luscious ingredients, are well known at the Chinese restaurant. Traditionally in China it was a dish served only in springtime to mark the reappearance of fresh produce. A soft pancake was served to the diners who put in their own fillings, rolled it and ate it, rather like Peking duck pancakes. The crispy restaurant version, wrapped in wonton or spring roll pastry is a delicious evolution. Here are its secrets.

The key to success is in the pastry. It must be the extremely thin Chinese spring roll pastry which is made from plain flour and water, and when deep fried goes cracklingly crisp. It is available frozen from Chinese and Asian stores and some delicatessens. The only substitute is Greek filo pastry, also available in packets from good delicatessens.

I give 8 filling variations, each with a common base which is explained below. The addition of further ingredient(s) produces the variation. You can save a few offcuts or leftovers from other dishes such as Peking Duck or Barbecued Pork to use in the filling.

Basic filling

2 tablespoons sesame oil
2 cloves garlic, peeled and finely
   chopped
1 inch (2.5 cm) cube ginger, peeled
   and finely chopped
2 spring onions, finely chopped
1 oz (25 g) Chinese mushroom,
   reconstituted (see page 146) and
   finely chopped
1 oz (25 g) carrot, finely shredded
1 oz (25 g) beansprouts

1 oz (25 g) mooli, finely shredded
1 tablespoon hoisin sauce
4 oz (110 g) your chosen filling
   variation (see pages 102–3)

Pastry

1 tablespoon cornflour
30 sheets spring roll pastry or filo
   pastry, each sheet being 10 inches
   (25cm) square

Basic filling

1. Heat the oil in a wok or frying pan. Stir-fry the garlic, ginger and spring onion for 2 minutes.

2. Add the mushrooms, carrot, beansprouts, mooli and hoisin sauce and stir-fry for a further 3–4 minutes.

3. Add one or more of your chosen variation ingredients listed below. Stir-fry for a further 2–3 minutes.

4. Remove the wok from the heat and allow to cool.

Making the roll

5. Mix the cornflour with water to make a paste. Set aside.

6. Spring roll (or filo) pastry needs careful handling. Being extremely thin it can dry out quickly and go brittle. To prevent this have a clean damp tea towel available. Open the packet and remove one sheet of pastry. Cover the packet with the tea towel.

7. Lay the sheet flat on a work surface.

8. Place about 3 tablespoons of filling on one corner of the sheet.

9. Spread it evenly over about 4 inches (10 cm).

10. Roll the sheet over the filling once.

11. Fold the sides in and over the covered filling.

12. Roll up reasonably tightly until a small triangle remains.

13. Brush some cornflour paste on the triangle and finish rolling up.

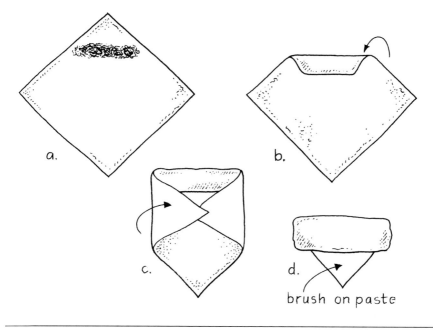

a.

b.

c.

d.

brush on paste

To cook Spring Rolls

14. Heat the deep-fryer to 375°F/190°C (chip-frying temperature).

15. Place no more than four spring rolls into the fryer at once (more will lower the oil temperature too much).

16. Cook for 8–10 minutes until golden.

17. Remove from the deep-fryer, shaking off the excess oil, and place on absorbent kitchen paper for a minute or two to drain. Keep warm while you fry the remaining spring rolls. Serve hot.

Note Spring roll pastry is usually sold frozen. Sheet size is normally 10 inches (25 cm) square and there are 30 sheets per pack. I find you can thaw the pack (it takes a couple of hours), remove what you need and refreeze the pack (wrap it first in cling film) without any harm coming to the sheets.

Complete spring rolls can be frozen. To re-heat from frozen follow the recipe above from stage 14.

Variations

Select a spring roll filling variation from below and add the appropriate ingredient(s) at stage 3 of the basic Spring Roll filling recipe on page 100.

BARBECUED PORK (CHAR SIU) SPRING ROLLS

Add 4 oz (110 g) finely shredded Barbecued Pork (see page 115).

PRAWN SPRING ROLLS

Add 4 oz (110 g) peeled prawns. If using frozen, thaw and drain first.

BEEF SPRING ROLLS

Add 4 oz (110 g) rump steak, that has been finely shredded (see page 23) then doused with 1 tablespoon dark soy sauce.

CHICKEN SPRING ROLLS

Add 4 oz (110 g) chicken breast fillet, skinned and finely shredded.

CRISPY DUCK SPRING ROLLS

When making the recipes on pages 119–123 reserve some offcuts for use in spring roll fillings. Add 4 oz (110 g) shredded crispy duck flesh.

SPECIAL MEAT SPRING ROLLS

Add 4 oz (110 g) total weight of any combination of the above meats and prawns to make your own personalised Special Meat Spring Rolls.

VEGETABLE SPRING ROLLS

Add the following ingredients to the basic spring roll filling.

1 oz (25 g) green beans, finely chopped
1 oz (25 g) canned or fresh pineapple pieces, finely chopped

1 oz (25 g) sweetcorn kernels
1 oz (25 g) frozen peas, thawed

SPECIAL VEGETABLE SPRING ROLLS

Add the following ingredients to the basic spring roll filling.

1 oz (25 g) water chestnuts, finely chopped
1 oz (25 g) bamboo shoot slices, finely chopped

1 oz (25 g) celery, finely chopped
1 oz (25 g) Chinese leaves, finely shredded
1 tablespoon plum sauce

STIR-FRY MEAT DISH FAVOURITES

Serves 4

These four stir-fried meat dishes are especially popular at the Chinese restaurant. Each starts with the same stir-fry base of marinated meat, but the
addition of particular ingredients makes each quite distinctive. The meat
used can be beef, lamb, pork, duck or chicken and an important key to
success is the marinating of the meat. Note the rather unusual use of custard
powder and fruit juice in the marinade – one of the little known tricks of the
restraurant trade and a jealously guarded secret.

Marinade
1 tablespoon hoisin sauce
2 tablespoons Chinese yellow rice
   wine or dry sherry
1 teaspoon orange juice
$\frac{1}{2}$ teaspoon custard powder

1 lb (450 g) trimmed lean meat, eg.
   rump, fillet or topside of beef, leg of
   lamb, leg of pork, skinless duck or
   chicken breast

2 tablespoons light vegetable oil
1–2 cloves garlic, peeled and finely
   chopped
6 spring onions, sliced
2 oz (50 g) canned sliced bamboo
   shoots, quartered
additions of your choice (see below and
   opposite)
a little stock, water or sherry

1. Mix the marinade ingredients together in a large bowl. Set aside for it
to blend well while you prepare the meat.

2. Cut the meat into thin slices about $1\frac{1}{2}$ inches (3.25 cm) × 1 inch
(2.5 cm) × $\frac{1}{4}$ inch (6 mm).

3. Immerse the meat in the marinade, and leave in the fridge for a minimum
of 1 hour and a maximum of 24 hours.

4. Heat the oil in a wok or frying pan. Stir-fry the garlic for 20–30 seconds.
Add the marinated meat piece by piece quickly, keeping the heat in the
wok quite hot. Stir frequently until all the meat is in the wok.

5. Add the spring onions and bamboo shoots and the special ingredients
of your choice (see opposite).

6. Add a little stock, water or sherry if required, to prevent major sticking,
but keep the dish fairly dry. Stir-fry until the meat is cooked to your
liking. This could be as little as 4 minutes or as long as 10 depending
on the meat of your choice and its cut. Poultry should be cooked until
opaque. Test a piece of meat to make sure it is cooked in the middle.
Serve as soon as it is ready.

Variations

For the following favourite restaurant stir-fries add the given ingredients at stage 5 of the basic recipe opposite.

STIR-FRY MEAT WITH GREEN PEPPERS AND BLACK BEAN SAUCE

1 green pepper, sliced or cut into long narrow diamond shapes

2 oz (50 g) onion, peeled and coarsely chopped

1 tablespoon black bean sauce

1 teaspoon granulated sugar

STIR-FRY MEAT WITH SZECHWAN HOT CHILLI

$1\frac{1}{2}$ inch (3.75 cm) cube fresh ginger, peeled and cut into thin julienne strips

4–6 fresh green chillies, chopped

1 red pepper, cut into small dice

$\frac{1}{2}$ teaspoon Chinese five-spice powder

STIR-FRY MEAT WITH SWEET PICKLED GINGER

Pickled ginger can be purchased in jars and it is quite delicious. Alternatively you can make it by following the recipe on page 46. Add 2 oz (50 g) of the strained pickled ginger at stage 5 of the basic stir-fry recipe.

STIR-FRY MEAT WITH PINEAPPLE AND CASHEW NUTS

4 slices fresh or canned pineapple, cut into wedges or cubes

2 oz (50 g) cashew nuts

1 teaspoon granulated sugar

SIZZLING DISHES

These are one of the spectacles of the Chinese restaurant scene. The particular dish is brought to the table on an oval cast iron platter, seated on a wooden base. The dish sizzles loudly and emits a considerable amount of aromatic steam. This particular piece of showmanship is not popular with all Chinese restaurant clients, however, as it can splutter small beads of oil over the diners. It has nothing to do with authentic culinary China either, but for those who wish to know the secrets of how it's done, here goes.

If you want to create sizzling dishes, it is essential to equip yourself with a sizzler as described above. These are available from some kitchen shops, or by post from The Curry Club (see page 181).

Practically any ingredient or dish can be 'sizzled'. It must be fully cooked first, so follow the recipe of your choice to its end then continue as follows.

1. Prior to serving, heat the cast iron sizzler directly on the stove (it works equally well on gas or electric).

2. When it is very hot and immediately prior to serving, put a little oil into the sizzler and add the hot pre-cooked ingredients. Keep the sizzler on the stove to ensure everything is piping hot.

3. Finally, and literally just as you serve it, squeeze some lemon juice into the sizzler. Hot oil and lemon juice react (quite actively) to create the steaming and sizzling. Serve to a round of applause.

CHAPTER 6

✥

MEAT SPECIALITY DISHES

This chapter contains a very varied selection of meat speciality dishes. I had a great deal of fun selecting them from some 200 menus from the best Chinese restaurants in the world. It was also frustrating and hard to confine my choice to just 12 dishes. It could easily have been 112, so great was the choice.

The final criteria in my selection were contrasting ingredients, contrasting techniques, intriguing titles and a combination of popular dishes and rarities. The ingredients include not only beef and pork, of course, but also the less commonly used lamb and rabbit.

Techniques include shredding, mincing, stir-frying, stewing, baking, twice cooking and barbecuing.

Whether well known or not, all of these dishes not only appear on the menus of Chinese restaurants somewhere in the world, but they are also traditional and authentic Chinese dishes.

TIGER'S WHISKERS

Serves 4

Some Chinese dishes have such wonderful names. This is one of my favourites. The dish has nothing to do with tigers other than that the finely shredded meat and vegetables represent the animal's whiskers, but the name evokes marvellous images. This dish can be cooked wet (with the addition of stock or water) or dry. I give the methods for both below. Fine shredding of both meat and vegetables is an important Chinese technique. See page 23 for instructions on shredding meat and vegetables.

3–4 tablespoons soy or sunflower oil
1 lb (450 g) best cut of lean beef such
   as topside or rump steak (weighed
   after trimming), shredded
1½ inch (3.75 cm) cube fresh ginger,
   peeled and shredded
2 cloves garlic, peeled and finely
   chopped

4 spring onions, coarsely chopped
1 tablespoon dark soy sauce
2 fl oz (50 ml) chicken or vintage
   master stock or water
2 oz (50 g) carrot, shredded
2 oz (50 g) beansprouts
2 oz (50 g) mangetout, shredded
spicy salt to taste

1. Heat 2 tablespoons of oil in a wok or frying pan.

2. Add about one quarter of the meat shreds and stir-fry fairly vigorously until the meat separates and is beginning to cook – about 1 minute. Stir less vigorously for a further minute.

3. Remove the meat from the wok, drain and keep warm.

4. Repeat stages 2 and 3 above, until all the meat is cooked, re-using the oil for the remaining batches of meat and adding more oil as needed.

5. Replenish the oil and stir-fry the ginger and garlic for 1 minute.

6. Add the spring onions and continue stir-frying for a further 2–3 minutes.

7. Add the soy sauce and the stock or water and stir-fry for a couple of minutes until it reduces and thickens a little.

8. Add the carrot, beansprouts and mangetout and stir-fry briskly for 1 minute.

9. Add in the still warm cooked meat and stir-fry until it is hot. Season to taste with spicy salt and serve.

Dry-cooked Tiger's Whiskers

This variation of the previous recipe simply omits the soy sauce and stock (i.e. stage 7 above) to produce a drier dish. Take care the ingredients don't stick when carrying out stage 8.

SHANGHAI LION'S HEAD

Serves 4

After the tiger, enter the lion! Called *shih tzu tou* in Chinese, these are large minced-pork balls which originated in Zhejiang in Eastern China. This very traditional version of the dish cooks the meat balls with Chinese leaves.

1 lb (450 g) leg of pork, weighed after boning and trimming
2–4 cloves of garlic, peeled and finely chopped
1 inch (2.5 cm) cube fresh ginger, peeled and finely chopped
1 teaspoon ten-spice powder
cornflour for rolling

1 tablespoon soy or light vegetable oil
4–6 spring onions, finely chopped
1¾ pints (1 litre) chicken or vintage master stock
8 oz (225 g) Chinese leaves, chopped into strips
salt to taste

1. Finely mince the pork with the garlic, ginger and ten-spice powder. Better still pulse it in a food processor to create a thick glutinous paste.

2. Divide the meat into 16 equal-sized lumps and roll them in a minimum amount of cornflour into balls or rissole shapes.

3. Heat the oil in a wok or frying pan. Stir-fry the spring onion for 2–3 minutes.

4. Add the stock and bring to the boil. Carefully place about 8 of the balls into the liquid and bring back to a simmer. Turn the balls if needed to ensure they are are starting to cook. After 1 minute they should begin to go firm.

5. Add the remaining 8 balls. Keep the stock on the simmer, stirring occasionally.

6. After about another 5 minutes add the Chinese leaves. Simmer for another 5 minutes or so, stirring occasionally.

7. Add salt to taste.

FILLET STEAK MANDARIN STYLE

Serves 4

Beef steak is an expensive luxury item and it always has been. Chinese emperors enjoyed steak, and here is an excellent recipe from the Mandarin royal court. It uses mandarins or oranges to achieve its distinctive flavour. Use only best-quality cuts of meat.

4 rump, fillet or sirloin steaks, each
  weighing 6 oz (175 g) when
  trimmed
1 teaspoon soy or light vegetable oil

Marinade
4 tablespoons Chinese yellow rice
  wine
3 tablespoons hoisin sauce
1 tablespoon plum sauce
1 tablespoon light soy sauce
1 teaspoon brown sugar
$\frac{1}{2}$ teaspoon ten-spice powder
juice of 2 mandarins or 1 orange

1. Lightly beat each steak with a meat mallet just a few times.

2. Mix together the marinade ingredients in a bowl.

3. Put the steaks in the marinade, turning them so they are coated totally. Cover and put in the fridge for a minimum of 3 hours and a maximum of 12 hours.

4. Heat the oil in a flat frying pan and stir-fry the steak until it is cooked to your liking. Serve with a rice or noodle dish.

PEKINESE BEEF STEW

Serves 4

We tend to think of most Chinese dishes being cooked fairly rapidly in the wok. Here is a traditional ancient stewing technique from North East China, in particular Beijing (or Peking). The sweet sauce is typical of the region. It must be stir-fried first in order to blend the flavourings effectively. The traditional way to cook this dish would be to slow-cook it for several hours in a wok. We can obtain equally good results much more quickly and more easily by casseroling it in the oven.

4 tablespoons vegetable oil
4–8 cloves garlic, peeled and finely chopped
4 oz (110 g) onion, peeled and finely chopped
1 lb (450 g) stewing steak, weighed after trimming
2 oz (50 g) sweet potato, peeled and chopped
1 oz (25 g) Chinese dried mushrooms

1 tablespoon red bean paste
1 tablespoon dark soy sauce
2 tablespoons hoisin sauce
1 tablespoon brown sugar
4 fl oz (110 ml) chicken or vintage master stock
further stock or water if necessary
2 fl oz (50 ml) Chinese yellow rice wine
spicy salt to taste

1. Heat the oven to 325°F/160°C/Gas 3.

2. Heat the oil in a wok or frying pan. Stir-fry the garlic and onion for about 3 minutes.

3. Add the meat and stir-fry for 5–6 minutes.

4. Transfer the contents of the wok to a lidded casserole dish. Add all the remaining ingredients except the wine and salt. Place into the oven.

5 Inspect after 20 minutes. Stir and add further stock or water if it needs it. Return to the oven.

6. Repeat stage 6 until the meat is tender. Total cooking time will be about 1–1¼ hours.

7. Add the wine and salt to taste and reheat. When hot it is ready to serve. Accompany with rice or noodles.

THREE MEATS WITH SPRING ONION

Serves 4

Meats in combination are a traditional Chinese technique and the results are exceptionally good. Occasionally you will come across this dish at the Chinese restaurant and it is well worth trying. Here I have used ham, beef and chicken.

8 oz (225 g) rump steak, trimmed
8 oz (225 g) skinless chicken breast
   meat
8 oz (225 g) cooked ham or Parma
   ham, trimmed
1 tablespoon soy or light vegetable oil
2 cloves garlic, peeled and finely
   chopped
1 inch (2.5 cm) cube fresh ginger,
   peeled and cut into strips

1 bunch spring onions, chopped
1 teaspoon five-spice powder
$\frac{1}{2}$ red pepper, cut into strips
$\frac{1}{2}$ green pepper, cut into strips
3 tablespoons Chinese yellow rice
   wine or dry sherry
salt to taste

1. Cut the three meats into thin strips or small $\frac{3}{4}$ inch (2 cm) cubes keeping the ham separate.

2. Heat the oil in a wok or frying pan. Stir-fry the garlic and ginger for 1 minute. Add the spring onions and five-spice powder and stir-fry for a further minute.

3. Add the beef and chicken and stir-fry for a couple of minutes to seal the meat.

4. Now add the ham, peppers, wine and salt to taste. Cook for about 5 minutes or until the beef is cooked to your liking, stirring occasionally.

STIR-FRIED PEKINESE MINCED PORK

Serves 4

Pork is China's favourite meat. It is often minced and is perfect for stir-frying in this form as it cooks very quickly.

$1\frac{1}{2}$ lb (675 g) boneless leg of pork, weighed after trimming

2 tablespoons soy or light vegetable oil

2–4 cloves of garlic, peeled and finely chopped

2 inch (5 cm) cube fresh ginger, peeled and finely chopped

3–4 spring onions, finely chopped

1 tablespoon finely chopped red pepper (optional)

2–3 fresh green chillies, finely chopped (optional)

1 tablespoon finely chopped fresh Chinese parsley or coriander (optional)

salt to taste

1. Roughly cut the pork into smallish chunks then mince it in a hand or electric mincer. I prefer a coarse mince but if you prefer it fine then put the mince through the mincer once or twice more.

2. Heat the oil in a wok or frying pan. Stir-fry the garlic and ginger for about 20 seconds. Add the spring onions and the optional red pepper and/or chilli and the Chinese parsley and stir fry for a couple of minutes until soft.

3. Add the minced pork and break it up by using a continuous stir-fry action. Fry for about 10 minutes. If it starts to stick add a minute amount of water.

4. Season to taste and serve.

TWICE-COOKED PORK

Serves 4

Twice cooking is a venerable and very ancient Chinese technique. A cheaper cut of meat such as belly of pork is first casseroled in stock, then it is marinated, diced and stir-fried. The result is a mature and very excellent dish.

2 lb (900 g) belly of pork, weighed after stage 1

1¾ pints (1 litre) chicken, vintage master or vegetable stock, or water with a chicken or vegetable stock cube

1 tablespoon soy or light vegetable oil

1 inch (2.5 cm) cube fresh ginger, peeled and finely chopped

2 cloves garlic, peeled and finely chopped

2–4 tablespoons Chinese yellow rice wine or sweet sherry

2 oz (50 g) beansprouts (optional)

1. The pork will come with bone and fat. Cut into three or four pieces, leave the bones and skin but trim off any excess fat.

2. Heat the stock in a 5-pint (3-litre) casserole dish. Heat the oven to 375°F/190°C/Gas 5. When the stock boils, remove the dish from the heat, add the pork, cover and put into the oven.

3. After about 35 minutes, test to see whether the meat is tender. If not, leave to cook until it is.

4. When tender drain off the remaining stock and allow the meat to cool. (Return the stock to your stock pot for future use, if liked.)

5. Cut up the pork into 1-inch (2.5 cm) cubes, again discarding any surplus fat and unwanted matter.

6. Heat the oil in a wok or frying pan.

7. Add the ginger and garlic and stir-fry for about 20 seconds. Add the cooked diced pork and stir-fry briskly for 3–4 minutes until it turns golden.

8. Add just enough wine to sizzle in the pan without swamping the meat. Add the optional beansprouts at this stage. Toss to heat through and serve immediately.

BARBECUED PORK

Serves 4

A trip through Chinatown is a wonderful experience at any time. The sights and smells, of which one is particularly enticing, are out of this world. Barbecued pork, or *char-siu*, is often prepared in view. Long lean fillets of pork are steeped in a bright red marinade, then roasted. They are cross cut into thin slices so that the white meat in the centre contrasts dazzlingly with the crispy red exterior.

Request lean pork fillets from your butcher. These should be around 8 inches (20 cm) long with a minimum thickness of $1\frac{1}{2}$ inches (4 cm).

2 pork fillets, each weighing about 12 oz (375 g) after trimming

Marinade
2 tablespoons honey
2 tablespoons red Chinese wine
1 tablespoon brown sugar
1 tablespoon light soy sauce

1 tablespoon hoisin sauce
2 teaspoons red Chinese vinegar
1 teaspoon red bean paste
1 teaspoon garlic powder
$\frac{1}{2}$ teaspoon ten-spice powder
a pinch red food colouring powder (optional)

1. Ensure that the fillets are free of all fat, gristle and bone.

2. Mix the marinade ingredients together in a large mixing bowl. Immerse the pork fillets in the marinade, cover the bowl and put it in the fridge for a minimum of 12 hours and a maximum of 24. Inspect and turn once or twice, if possible.

3. Heat the oven to 375°F/190°C/Gas 5.

4. Drain the fillets, reserving the marinade.

5. Place the fillets on a wire rack in an oven tray. Bake for 15 minutes. Turn and baste with reserved marinade. Bake for a further 10 minutes. Turn and baste again. Bake for about 5 more minutes.

6. Test that the meat is cooked by cutting off one end. If it is, cut the fillets across the grain into $\frac{1}{4}$ inch (6 mm) discs. Serve hot.

BARBECUED SPARE RIBS

Serves 4

These are one of the more popular products of the Chinese restaurant. They make an excellent starter (see also page 67) or a second course between starter and main course. Why they are called 'spare' ribs is a mystery.

Ask your butcher for pork spare ribs and he will chop them into single ribs for you. Most restaurants serve them this way, but you can get them cross-cut to form small pieces about 1 inch (2.5 cm) across.

16 pork spare ribs, total weight
  2–2½ lb (900–1.1 kg)

Marinade
4–6 tablespoons hoisin sauce
2–3 tablespoons Chinese yellow rice
  wine or sweet sherry

1. Thin the hoisin sauce with Chinese rice wine or sherry. Aim for a loose marinade sauce.

2. Coat the ribs with the marinade, cover and put in the fridge for a minimum of 3 hours and a maximum of 12 hours .

3. Heat the oven to 375°F/190°C/Gas 5.

4. Place the ribs on a wire rack in an oven tray and put into the oven. Reserve any spare marinade. Bake for 10–15 minutes, basting with the spare marinade once or twice. They should be crispy and cooked by then; if not cook for a while longer. Serve at once.

SZECHWAN SPARE RIBS

This is a delightfully spicy-hot variation of the previous recipes from the Szechwan province. The quantity of ribs and the method is the same, only the marinade ingredients are different.

Marinade
2–3 tablespoons hoisin sauce
1–3 tablespoons chilli and garlic sauce

1–2 tablespoons Chinese yellow rice
  wine or dry sherry

PEKINESE GLAZED SPARE RIBS

Serves 4

This version of spare ribs has a sweetness that is typical of Northern China.

16 pork spare ribs, total weight
2–2½ lb (900 g–1.1 kg)

Marinade
2–3 tablespoons hoisin sauce
½ tablespoon red or black bean sauce
2–3 tablespoons Chinese yellow rice
wine or sweet sherry

1 tablespoon brown sugar
½ teaspoon five-spice powder

Glaze
4 tablespoons clear honey
1 tablespoon Worcestershire sauce

1. Mix the marinade ingredients together.

2. Coat the ribs with the marinade, cover and put in the fridge for a minimum of 3 hours and a maximum of 12 hours.

3. Heat the oven to 375°F/190°C/Gas 5. Mix the glaze ingredients together.

4. Put the ribs on a wire rack in an oven tray and coat with the glaze.

5. Bake for 10–15 minutes, basting with the glaze once or twice. The ribs should be crispy and cooked by then; if not cook for a while longer. Serve at once.

CHAPTER 7

POULTRY AND GAME
SPECIALITY DISHES

The recipes in this chapter fall into three categories – duck, chicken and game dishes. Again I had great difficulty making my selection from the vast range of restaurant dishes on offer.

One thing was certain, I had to include Peking Duck; this book would be naked without it. In my view, and evidently that of the emperors of the fabulous Ming dynasty, it is probably China's most supreme dish. I make no apology therefore for a lengthy method and recipe. To make up for it, I have also given two really quick alternative recipes for duck which can be served in the same way with pancakes, hoisin sauce and shredded cucumber and spring onions.

The five chicken dishes give a varied selection of tastes including the delightfully named Pekinese Drunken Chicken, which is cooked in rice wine.

The Chinese have many recipes involving wild birds and game and I have included two – Deep-Fried Hong Kong Pigeon, a simple but highly effective dish and Yankzee Rabbit.

PEKING DUCK TRADITIONAL STYLE

Serves 4

The emperors of China's most opulent Ming dynasty (1368–1644) demanded the best of everything at their Peking imperial court. Their chefs were not immune from such edicts and they too were expected to invent culinary masterpieces, of which many had become classics by the sixteenth century. Of these, Peking Duck must be the most well known and loved.

Until recently the food at the Chinese restaurant in the West was the relatively bland fare from Canton. It was not until the 1960s that Pekinese food burst upon the West with a glamour and novelty that occurs from time to time. I remember my first exciting venture into Peking style eating took place at the Richmond Rendezvous restaurant in West London. The highlight was Peking Duck. Now the sight and aroma of part-cooked, chestnut-red ducks hanging up to dry is almost commonplace in the Chinatowns throughout the West.

Most Chinese restaurants offer Peking Duck as a menu highlight. It can be taken as a starter, second course or as part of a main course. It must be served and eaten in the traditional manner or it simply isn't the same. There are four components: small thin wheat 'pancakes', cooked and brought to the table in a bamboo steamer; a side plate of finely shredded spring onions and cucumber; a small bowl of hoisin sauce; and the duck (or part duck) on the bone. The flesh and skin are carved or shredded into chopstick-sized pieces at the table and it must be cooked well enough to fall off the bone. The skin must be crackling crisp and there must be no fat left. To achieve this, the traditional and rather laborious cooking preparation must be adhered to, and started hours ahead. So I'm afraid I'm going to make you work for this recipe.

The original and traditional way the duck was used reflects the thrifty ways of the Chinese. Only the crispy skin was used with the pancakes. The flesh was used for another dish at the same meal. The bones and offcuts went into the stock pot. You can follow this concept if you wish.

The eating of this dish also follows a traditional ritual. Each diner takes a pancake from the steamer, and places it on a side plate. It is smeared with hoisin sauce upon which is then placed a little duck and some spring onion and cucumber shreds. The pancake is rolled up and hey presto, you have a delicious gastronomic experience. The Chinese are deftly able to do all this with chopsticks but most of us use our fingers or a combination of chopsticks and fingers. A finger bowl for each diner is a final touch – float a flower petal in it for effect. This dish makes a great talking point when you're entertaining. One final observation – this dish really must be eaten on its own as a separate course or meal in order to get the most from it.

In the traditional method of preparing Peking Duck it is important to separate the duck's skin from its body before cooking it. To do so, you'll need a whole plucked duck with its neck and head intact (your butcher should be able to oblige if you give him plenty of notice). This enables you to separate the skin at stage 3. If you want to omit this operation and use an ordinary neckless oven-ready duck you can. The result will be almost as good but more fatty. Simply omit stage 3.

1 duck with head on weighing
  around 4 lb (1.8 kg)

Coating sauce
6 fl oz (175 ml) hoisin sauce
2 tablespoons Chinese yellow rice
  wine or dry sherry
1 tablespoon brown sugar
4 tablespoons runny honey
1 teaspoon ginger juice (optional)
1 teaspoon spicy salt
½ teaspoon beetroot powder

To serve
16 pancakes (see opposite)
hoisin sauce
half a cucumber, peeled and cut into
  julienne
4–6 spring onions, cut into julienne

1. Boil a large pan of water. Immerse the duck in it for 20–30 seconds. Remove and cool, discarding the water. Wash the duck inside and out then rinse it. Boil a pan of fresh water then immerse the duck in it for 20–30 seconds. Remove it and thoroughly dry it. Discard the water.

2. Place the duck on a rack in a warmer or an oven at its lowest setting. Switch off the warmer or oven after an hour and leave the duck for a couple more hours at least.

3. Now you can optionally separate the skin from the flesh. The restaurants use a small hose attached to a compressor. At home you will have to use a drinking straw. It needs a bit of puff and patience but it does work. Make a small incision in the skin just large enough to take the straw at the base of the duck's neck. Insert the straw and blow little and often. The skin should come away all around the duck. Cut off the neck and use for stock.

4. Place the coating sauce ingredients in a pan and stir over a gentle heat until the sugar and honey have dissolved.

5. Coat the dry duck skin with the coating sauce. Repeat stage 2. (In China and Chinatown they hang the ducks to dry in a warm place – you can do this if you wish.) After drying it should be a beautiful chestnut red colour and it could have taken as little as 4–6 hours to reach this stage, or overnight if you prefer.

6. Heat the oven to 375°F/190°C/Gas 5. If you have a spit roast device place the duck centrally on the skewer and spit roast for about $1-1\frac{1}{4}$ hours. Otherwise place the duck on its front on a wire rack over an oven tray. Roast for 25 minutes. Turn the duck the other way up and roast for a further 25 minutes. Turn back for 10 more minutes and back again (so that it is front up) for a final 10–20 minutes. It does not need basting.

7. During the last few minutes of roasting, steam the pancakes (see below).

8. Transfer the duck to a large serving dish, take to the table and carve or shred (using two forks and a pulling motion) into chopstick-sized pieces. Serve with the hot pancakes, hoisin sauce and julienne strips of cucumber and spring onion.

Note: Restaurants use red food colouring and monosodium glutamate (MSG) instead of beetroot powder to obtain the deep red colour of the duck.

PANCAKES

Makes 16 pancakes

These can be purchased frozen from Chinese stores. They are ready to serve after a few minutes steaming (follow stages 6, 7 and 8 of the method below). Alternatively make them yourself as follows. In fact they are not pancakes as we know them, which are made from batter, but are thin bread discs made from dough.

8 oz (225 g) strong white flour
water

1. Mix the flour with enough water to form a pliable dough.

2. Let it stand for 20 minutes or so.

3. Divide the dough into four equal parts, then each of those into four to make 16. Form each into a ball.

4. Take one ball and roll it out on a floured board into a thin disc about $5\frac{1}{2}$ inches (14 cm) in diameter.

5. Place under a clean, damp tea towel while you roll out the remaining 15 balls.

6. Set up a bamboo steamer over a pan or wok of boiling water (see page 97).

7. Stack the pancakes one on top of the other and place in the steamer tray. Cover and steam them for a couple of minutes.

8. Serve promptly as they harden off rather fast.

PEKING DUCK (Fast Method)

Serves 4

Here is a method for cooking Peking Duck which omits all the tedious and time-consuming processes given in the previous recipe. It simply uses best duck breast – ask for *magrets de canard.*

2 duck breasts, about 8 oz (225 g) each
4–5 tablespoons hoisin sauce

To serve
16 pancakes (see page 121)

hoisin sauce
half a cucumber, peeled and cut into julienne
4–6 spring onions, cut into julienne

1. Heat the oven to 325°F/170°C/Gas 3.

2. Cover an oven tray with kitchen foil. Put the breasts skin side up on the foil. Put the tray into the oven.

3. Remove after 15–20 minutes. Allow to cool enough for you to be able to remove the skin and fat. Drain off all liquid.

4. Coat the top and bottom of the breasts generously with hoisin sauce. Replace on the foil and put back into the oven.

5. Cook for a further 20 minutes then inspect and baste with more hoisin sauce.

6. Increase the oven temperature to 350°F/180°C/Gas 4 and cook for a final 10–15 minutes.

7. Remove and allow to cool to handling stage, then shred as finely as you wish (using two forks and a pulling motion). The sauce should be dry enough to make this process easy. The duck should still be warm enough to serve, but if necessary return it to the oven for a short re-heat.

8. Serve with pancakes, hoisin sauce, cucumber and spring onions as for the previous recipe.

SZECHWAN DUCK

Serves 4

This is a variation of the previous recipe and it is equally fast. Traditionally Szechwan Duck is served with steamed buns (see Glossary) and Chinese ten-spice powder. However it is just as good (but a lot less bother) if served with rice or noodles

4 duck breasts, each weighing about
  8 oz (225 g)
1–2 tablespoons Szechwan chilli
  sauce

1 tablespoon plum sauce
2 tablespoons hoisin sauce
1 teaspoon ten-spice powder

1. Proceed with stages 1, 2 and 3 of the previous recipe.

2. Mix the sauces and powder together. Coat the top and bottom of the breasts with this mixture. Replace the breasts on the foil and put the oven tray back in the oven.

3. Continue with stages 5 to 7 of the previous recipe, using the sauce and powder mixture to baste the duck, and slicing it thinly rather than shredding it in stage 7.

ROAST DUCK WITH CHESTNUTS

Serves 4

This dish can be approached in two ways. Either use the flesh from a prepared Peking Duck (see page 119) or roast a duck specifically for this dish. The recipe below uses a standard oven roast technique. The cavity and skin are rubbed with vinegar and Chinese ten-spice powder before it is roasted. Then, towards the end of cooking time it is stuffed with a mixture of sweet chestnuts and water chestnuts.

1 duck weighing around 4 lb (1.8 kg)
Chinese white rice vinegar for rubbing
ten-spice powder for rubbing

Stuffing
14 oz (400 g) canned sweet chestnuts,
*   drained, or chestnut purée*
8 oz (225 g) canned water chestnuts,
*   drained*
1 teaspoon ten-spice powder

1. Wash the duck inside and out and dry it with absorbent kitchen paper.

2. Rub the cavity and the outside of the duck first with the vinegar then liberally with the ten-spice powder.

3. Let it stand while the oven heats to 375°F/190°C/Gas 5.

4. Put the duck on to a spit roast device, if your oven has one, and spit roast for about 40 minutes. Alternatively place it breast-down on a wire rack over an oven tray and roast for 20 minutes. Turn the duck the other way up and roast for a further 20 minutes.

5. Meanwhile prepare the stuffing. Mash the sweet chestnuts and chop the water chestnuts into smallish cubes. Mix the two together along with the ten-spice powder.

6. Withdraw the duck from the oven or spit at the end of stage 4. Allow it to cool enough to drain off excess fat from the drip tray and the cavity.

7. Put the stuffing into the cavity. Return the duck to the spit and roast for another 20–40 minutes, or return it to the oven and roast on both sides for 10–20 minutes a side.

8. When it is fully cooked, slice it and serve it with the stuffing.

EASTERN CHINA BRAISED DUCK

Serves 4

Use plump duck breasts (*magrets de canard*) for this simple dish from Central-eastern China.

4 duck breasts (*magret du canard*)
  each weighing about 6 oz (175 g)
cornflour for dipping
oil for deep-frying and stir-frying
2 cloves garlic, peeled and finely
  chopped

$\frac{1}{2}$ *pint (300 ml) chicken or other stock*
1 tablespoon dark soy sauce
4 tablespoons Chinese yellow rice
  wine or sweet sherry
spicy salt to taste

1. Cut the breasts into slices $1\frac{1}{2}$–2 inches (3.75–5 cm) long by $\frac{1}{2}$ inch (1.25 cm) thick.

2. Heat the deep-fryer to 375°F/190°C (chip-frying temperature).

3. Dip half the duck slices in the cornflour and place them straight away into the deep-fryer. This is done in more than one batch to ensure that the fryer's temperature is maintained.

4. Fry for 5 minutes.

5. Remove from the deep-fryer and shake off excess oil. Keep warm while you deep-fry the remaining duck slices.

6. Heat a little oil in a wok and stir-fry the garlic for 20 seconds.

7. Add the stock and soy sauce and when boiling, the duck pieces.

8. Simmer for 10 more minutes or until the meat is to your liking.

9. Add the wine or sherry at the last minute with spicy salt to taste, and when the dish is simmering, serve.

WALNUT CHICKEN

The combination of nuts and chicken in a light sauce is a Chinese restaurant speciality. Many variations are possible including almond, pine nut, cashew nut or peanut chicken.

4 spring onions, chopped
1 tablespoon soy or light vegetable oil
1 lb (450 g) skinless chicken breast fillets
1 tablespoon yellow bean paste

10 pieces red pepper, cut into diamonds
1 oz (25 g) shelled walnuts, chopped
2–3 tablespoons Chinese yellow rice wine, sweet sherry, stock or water
spicy salt to taste

1. Dice the chicken breast fillets into bite-sized cubes.

2. Heat the oil in a wok or frying pan. Add the spring onions and stir-fry for 1 minute.

3. Add the chicken pieces and stir-fry briskly for 2–3 minutes.

4. Add the yellow bean paste and enough water to prevent the chicken pieces sticking and fry for 5 minutes, stirring from time to time.

5. Add the red pepper diamonds and the walnuts. Stir-fry for about 5 more minutes, adding the wine, sherry, stock or water during this stage to keep things in motion. Add salt to taste.

HOT SPICY CHICKEN

Serves 4

This is one of those instant stir-fry dishes which make Chinese food so fresh and alive. In this simple recipe from Guizhou, a south-western Chinese province, it is the combination of chilli heat from the West and sweet and sour from the South which gives the thin slices of chicken breast their unique flavour.

2 tablespoons soy or light vegetable oil
1 lb (450 g) chicken breasts, skinned and boned
custard powder for dipping
1 tablespoon red bean paste
1 tablespoon chilli and garlic sauce

1 tablespoon brown sugar
2 tablespoons sweet and sour sauce (see page 86)
2 oz (50 g) pak-choi (Chinese cabbage), chopped
spicy salt to taste

1. Heat the oil in a wok or frying pan.

2. Dip one chicken breast in the custard powder. Cut it into thin $\frac{1}{4}$ inch (6 mm) slices (not shreds).

3. Place the slices straight away into the wok and stir-fry briskly.

4. Take the wok off the heat after 30 seconds. Repeat stage 2 with another chicken breast. Place the wok back on to the heat and stir-fry briskly for 30 seconds. Repeat this sequence until all the chicken is in the wok. The wok can get rather sticky during this stage so keep scraping it with a spoon – don't let it start to burn.

5. Add 1 tablespoon of water, then add the red bean paste, chilli and garlic sauce, sugar and the sweet and sour sauce.

6. When the contents of the wok are sizzling add a little more water to keep things moving, then add the chopped Chinese pak-choi.

7. Stir-fry until the chicken is cooked. Season to taste with spicy salt and serve.

PEKINESE DRUNKEN CHICKEN
—— · ——

Serves 4

This dish is famous for its name. It is in fact a traditional dish that dates back to the Tang dynasty (618–907 AD). It is said to have been created in honour of the emperor's beautiful mistress. She eventually fell from grace, but the dish lives on and over the centuries its name must have raised many a laugh, as it still does today. The chicken is simmered in a stock with as much alcohol as you care to add. There is, of course, a European equivalent to this dish – the French *coq au vin*.

The quantity of alcohol specified below is an average amount for you to increase or decrease as you require.

1 lb (450 g) chicken breasts, skinned
   and boned
2 tablespoons soy or light oil
4 spring onions, chopped
$\frac{1}{2}$ pint (300 ml) chicken stock

1 tablespoon sugar
$\frac{1}{2}$ pint (300 ml) Chinese yellow rice
   wine or sweet sherry
spicy salt to taste

1. Dice the chicken breasts into bite-sized cubes.

2. Heat the oil in a wok or frying pan. Add the onion and stir-fry for 1 minute.

3. Add the chicken pieces and stir-fry briskly for 2–3 minutes.

4. Add the stock and the sugar and bring to the simmer. Allow to simmer for about 10 minutes, stirring occasionally. The stock should reduce to a minimal amount without the chicken burning.

5. Add the Chinese rice wine and salt to taste. Return to the simmer and serve promptly.

Opposite VEGETARIAN MENU
Clockwise from the top: Marbled Eggs (page 73) and Fried Cashew Nuts (page 53) in Crispy Noodle Nests (page 52), Vegetable Fried Rice (page 168), Peking Dip Sauce (page 53), Stuffed Cucumber (page 155), Stuffed Black Mushrooms (page 151), and Sour Plums with Cherry Tomatoes and Celery (page 156). Note the wok cleaning brush, bottom left, and the small noodle nest maker, top left (see pages 20 and 21).

CANTONESE LEMON CHICKEN

Serves 4

From Hong Kong comes this delightful and popular Chinese restaurant dish. If ever there was a dish to exemplify the Yin and Yang of taste, colour and texture, this is it. Pieces of chicken breast are lightly coated with cornflour and deep-fried. They are then served with a sweet and sour lemon sauce.

1 lb(450 g) chicken breasts, skinned and boned
cornflour for dipping

½ teaspoon spicy salt
4 tablespoons custard powder

Sauce
juice of 2 lemons
1 tablespoon caster sugar
2 tablespoons Chinese yellow rice wine or white wine

Garnish
finely shredded carrot
finely chopped fresh parsley
lemon wedges

1. In a saucepan mix together the lemon juice, sugar, wine and spicy salt. Add the custard powder and enough water to make a thin paste. Mix well.

2. Put the saucepan on the stove and bring to the simmer, stirring continuously whilst it thickens to prevent it sticking. Add a little water as you go if it thickens too much. Aim for a thick but pourable sauce. When it stops thickening, set it aside but keep warm.

3. Heat the deep-fryer to 375°F/190°C (chip-frying temperature).

4. Cut the chicken breasts into bite-sized cubes.

5. Coat half the cubes in cornflour then place in the deep-fryer. Fry until golden – about 10–12 minutes is ample. Drain and keep warm.

6. Repeat stage 5 with the remaining cubes of chicken.

7. When you are ready to serve the dish, place the chicken cubes in a serving bowl and pour over the hot sauce. Garnish with the shredded carrot, chopped parsley and lemon wedges and serve immediately.

Opposite CANTONESE SPECIAL MENU
Clockwise from the top: Wonton Soup (page 60) in hand carved melon cup (page 177), Deep-fried Cellophane Noodles (page 159), Pickled Ginger (page 46), Snow-pea Stir-fry (page 154), Stir-fry Duck with Pineapple and Cashew Nuts (page 105), and Dragon's Teeth (page 153).

SEA SPICY or SALT-BAKED CHICKEN

Serves 4

Salt has been produced in Southern China for thousands of years. It has many culinary uses, including preserving. This recipe was developed during the Ching dynasty (1644–1912). The raw chicken is rubbed generously inside and out with spicy salt. It is then wrapped in kitchen foil (formerly a special paper would have been used) and oven baked.

The addition of oyster sauce and prawn powder adds a taste of the sea and gives a wonderful balance of Yin and Yang.

1 roasting chicken, weighing about
  2½–3 lb (1.1–1.4 kg)
spicy salt for rubbing and sprinkling
2 tablespoons soy or light vegetable
  oil
2–4 cloves of garlic, peeled and finely
  shredded
2 teaspoons white sesame seeds
2 tablespoons oyster sauce
2 teaspoons prawn powder

½ pint (300 ml) chicken or vintage
  master stock or water
2 oz (50 g) dried Chinese mushrooms,
  any type, reconstituted (see page
  146)
6 large leaves choy-sum (see page
  145) or spinach, chopped
2–3 tablespoons chopped spring onion
  leaves

1. Wash the chicken inside and out and roughly dry it with absorbent kitchen paper, so that it remains slightly damp.

2. Make small slashes in the skin with a sharp knife.

3. Using kitchen gloves rub spicy salt generously inside and outside the chicken.

4. Heat the oven to 375°F/190°C/Gas 5.

5. Wrap the chicken in foil then place it on its side on a wire rack over an oven tray. Put the oven tray into the oven.

6. Bake for 20 minutes. Remove from the oven and turn the chicken over on to its other side. Bake for a further 20 minutes.

7. Take the chicken out of the oven and remove the foil using oven gloves. Place the chicken on its front on the rack and sprinkle with some more spicy salt. Return it to the oven for 15 more minutes.

8. Meanwhile prepare the sauce. Heat the oil in a wok or frying pan. Stir-fry the garlic and sesame seeds for 10–15 seconds. Add the oyster sauce, the prawn powder and enough of the stock or water to keep the sauce from sticking. Stir-fry for 3–4 minutes.

9. Add the remaining stock and the Chinese mushrooms. Simmer until the end of stage 10.

10. Remove the chicken from the oven and turn on to its back. Bake for a final 10–15 minutes. The exact time must be determined by inspection and the prick test: insert the tip of a slim sharp knife or skewer into the thickest part of a thigh and if the juice runs out clear it is cooked.

11. Remove the bird from the oven and let it rest for 5 minutes or so. The outside should then be crispy. Carve the chicken into large sections.

12. Add the choy-sum or spinach and spring onion leaves to the sauce and when it simmers pour it over the chicken sections. Serve.

DEEP-FRIED HONG KONG PIGEON

Serves 4

I discovered this dish when on a business trip to Hong Kong. As a gastronomic centre Hong Kong cannot be bettered. There are dining establishments at all price levels and standards, from very expensive to incredibly cheap. I love them all, needless to say, and it does not have to be the dearest restaurant where one gets the best food. In Hong Kong cheap and cheerful food stalls abound. Some are truly excellent. They appear on every street, every corner and every open space. Most specialise in just one type of food. This is the recipe, as near as I can re-create it, from one of those stands.

4 oven-ready pigeons

Stock
2¼ pints (1.2 litres) chicken stock

4 tablespoons hoisin sauce
2 tablespoons tomato ketchup
1 teaspoon five-spice powder

1. Wash the pigeons inside and out.

2. Bring the stock ingredients to the boil in a saucepan. Place the pigeons in and reduce the heat to a low simmer.

3. Cook for about 45 minutes, inspecting from time to time. Test that the meat is tender by piercing it.

4. Remove the pigeons. Allow to cool then place in the fridge uncovered for 24 hours. This dries them effectively in preparation for stage 6.

5. Strain the stock liquid, discarding the solids. Store the liquid for future use in another recipe.

6. Bring the pigeons out of the fridge to return to room temperature about 1 hour before you fry them.

7. Shortly before serving, heat the deep-fryer to 375 °F/190°C (chip-frying temperature).

8. Ensure that the pigeons are dry, then carefully lower all four into the deep-fryer.

9. Cook for about 8 minutes, turning them once or twice.

10. Remove from the fryer, shaking off all excess oil. Rest them for a few minutes on a bed of absorbent kitchen paper – which will enable them to go crispy – then serve on their own or as part of a meal.

YANGTZE RABBIT

Serves 4

Rabbit is popular all over China, as are most forms of game. Rarely, if ever, is this acknowledged in the Chinese restaurants of the West.

1 lb (450 g) boneless rabbit meat, weighed after trimming
2 tablespoons soy or light vegetable oil
1 tablespoon cornflour

8 fl oz (250 ml) chicken or vintage master stock
1 tablespoon Chinese yellow rice wine or dry sherry
salt to taste

1. Thinly slice the meat, then cut it into shreds (see page 23).

2. Heat the oil in a wok or frying pan. Add the rabbit shreds and stir-fry for a couple of minutes to seal them.

3. Mix the cornflour into the stock and add to the wok. Stir-fry continuously until it will thicken no more. Ensure the heat is never too high or the mixture will catch and burn.

4. Add the wine or sherry and simmer for a few more minutes. Add salt to taste.

5. Serve with plain rice and beansprouts, if liked.

CHAPTER 8

SEAFOOD DISHES

I must say that if I have one criticism of the Chinese restaurant in the West it is its singularly unimaginative approach to seafood and fish dishes. Nearly all seem to confine their choice to small prawns, which are sprinkled into fried rice, spring roll fillings and chop suey, or the larger king prawns. Perhaps this is the fault of the diners. In the past the people of Great Britain, for example, were notorious for their lack of interest in the fruits of the sea, despite living on an island with many miles of coastline. China also has an enormous coast line that is thousands of miles long. China is also blessed with some major rivers, including the world's third longest river, the Yangtze, and the famous Yellow River. Much of China's territory is sub-tropical, including its waters, and this results in an abundance of seafood and freshwater fish.

My dishes I have chosen for this chapter include prawns, squid, oysters, clam, scallops, crab and fish. They are all authentic Chinese dishes each with its own history and they have all appeared at some time on the menu of various enlightened Chinese restaurants.

PEKING PHOENIX EMPEROR PRAWNS

Serves 4

The phoenix is a Chinese symbol of great importance. It represents reincarnation and positive thinking. It is depicted as a curious five-part beast with the head of a chicken, the long neck of an asp, the breast of a bird, the back of a turtle and the tail of a king prawn.

The imperial chefs would cook this dish to please their emperor master, and it was important that the prawns did not curl up. Consequently, they cut the underside of the prawn in the manner described below.

20–24 king prawns, weighing at least 1½ lb (675 g) when shelled
about 4 tablespoons soy or light vegetable oil
2 cloves of garlic, peeled and shredded
1 inch (2.5 cm) cube fresh ginger, peeled and shredded
1 tablespoon Chinese red or black vinegar
1 tablespoon brown sugar
1 tablespoon dark soy sauce

2 teaspoons tomato purée
2 tablespoons Chinese yellow rice wine or sweet sherry
juice of 2 tangerines

Garnish
a thick bunch of chives and/or the finely shredded green leaves of spring onions
spicy salt to taste
a few small white spring onion rings

1. If the prawns have their shells on, you have the option of leaving the tails on. Shell as required then wash carefully.

2. Cut lightly down the back of the king prawns and remove the vein. Turn the prawns over and cut along the underside, going a little deeper than before but not over half way down. Wash them again and dry them.

3. Heat some oil in a wok or frying-pan. Reduce the heat to medium. Stir-fry the prawns in two or three batches for about 5–8 minutes. Keep them flat and they will go a nice pink colour.

4. While the prawns are cooking make the sauce. Heat some more oil in another wok or pan. Stir-fry the garlic and ginger for 1 minute. Add the vinegar, brown sugar, soy sauce and tomato purée.

5. Stir-fry this so that it thickens and 'caramelises' but doesn't go too sticky. Add the wine and tangerine juice as the sauce begins to thicken and stir-fry for a couple more minutes.

6. Make a bed of chives and/or long finely shredded spring onion leaves on a serving plate. Place the prawns on top, all flattened and facing the same direction. Pour over the sauce, sprinkle with spicy salt and garnish with miniature spring onion rings.

SZECHWAN CHILLI PRAWNS

Serves 4

Although you can use frozen shelled prawns of any size for this dish, the best presentation is achieved by choosing fresh prawns with their shell on and of a reasonable size (about 50 to each 1 lb/450 g). They can then be carefully peeled but the tail left on. The pink colour of the prawns contrasts gorgeously with the green and/or red of the chillies.

$1\frac{1}{2}$ lb (675 g) fresh raw prawns with
   shell on (see above)
3 tablespoons soy or light vegetable
   oil
2–4 cloves garlic, peeled and puréed
2 oz (50 g) onion, peeled and finely
   chopped

2–4 fresh red and/or green chillies
0–2 teaspoons chilli powder
   (optional)
1 teaspoon five-spice powder
salt to taste

1. Peel the prawns but leave the tail on, then wash and dry them.

2. If necessary, cut lightly down the back of the prawns and remove the vein. Wash them again and dry them.

3. Heat the oil in a wok or frying pan. Stir-fry the garlic for 20 seconds. Add the onion and continue stir-frying for a further 3–4 minutes.

4. Add the chillies, optional chilli powder and the five-spice powder. Stir in well and when sizzling add enough water to make a thickish sauce.

5. Add the prawns and stir carefully for 10 minutes. Add water bit by bit as necessary to maintain the texture of the sauce.

6. Add salt to taste and serve.

FRIED SHREDDED SQUID

Serves 4

By shredding and deep-frying the squid this clever Szechwan recipe transforms them into succulent, golden, tasty food. The perfect contrast is achieved
by the addition of silver beansprout tails. The result is perfect Yin and Yang.

1 lb (450 g) squid
8 oz (225 g) very fresh white
beansprouts
2 tablespoons soy or light vegetable
oil
2–4 cloves garlic, peeled and finely
shredded
2 oz (50 g) onion, peeled and finely
shredded
2–4 fresh green chillies, chopped
(optional)

1 tablespoon chopped fresh coriander
leaves
1 teaspoon five-spice powder
1 tablespoon brown sugar
2 tablespoons Chinese white rice
vinegar
1 tablespoon light soy sauce
salt to taste

1. Wash the squid. Cut off the heads, and use for stock. Rinse the squid
   again and work out the ink. Cut them open and remove the quill. Rinse
   until the water runs quite clear. Dry. Cut the squid into strips the same
   length and thickness as the beansprouts.

2. Choose very white beansprouts. Cut off the bean ends and the tips.
   Discard or use for stock. Immerse the straight white tails in a bowl of
   cold water and leave until stage 6.

3. Heat the oil in a wok or frying pan. Stir-fry the garlic for 20 seconds.
   Add the onion and continue stir-frying for a further 3–4 minutes.

4. Add the optional chillies, the fresh coriander and the five-spice powder.
   Stir in well and add the sugar, vinegar and soy sauce and enough water
   to make a thickish sauce.

5. Add the squid and stir-fry carefully for 10–12 minutes. Add more water
   as necessary, bit by bit, to maintain the texture of the sauce.

6. Drain the beansprouts and add to the squid with salt to taste. Mix very
   well. Put the lid on the wok and leave for a few minutes to heat through
   before serving.

OYSTER BLACK BEANS

Serves 4

Oysters are quite common in China, making regular appearances in cooking, mainly in the form of oyster sauce. This particular recipe steams whole oysters very briefly, then mixes them with black beans in oyster sauce. They are served in their shells to make the maximum impact and can be served as a starter or second course on their own. If you can't get fresh oysters in the shell, use tinned or bottled oysters and steam and serve them in a dish, garnished with spring onion rings.

8 prepared oysters in their shell
1 tablespoon soy or vegetable oil
2 tablespoons black beans, lightly mashed
1 tablespoon oyster sauce
1 tablespoon light soy sauce
salt to taste

Garnish
lettuce leaves
mustard and cress

1. Set up a two- or three-deck bamboo steamer (see page 97) and when the water boils place the oysters in their shells into the steamer trays. Steam for 5–6 minutes.

2. Meanwhile, heat the oil in a wok or frying pan. Add the black beans, oyster sauce and the soy sauce.

3. When it is sizzling, add a little water to maintain a thick but fluid sauce. Add salt to taste.

4. At the end of stage 1, remove the oysters in shells from the steamer.

5. Carefully spoon some sauce into each shell then place the oysters on to a large serving plate, garnished with lettuce and mustard and cress. Serve at once.

Clam Red Beans

This is a variation of the previous recipe, using fresh clams in their shell instead of oysters and red beans in place of black in the sauce. You will need about 16 clams to serve 4 people as a starter or second course.

MONGOLIAN SCALLOPS

Serves 4

Inner Mongolia is in the north of China. Indeed it is north of the Chinese wall, and for thousands of years the various dynasties spent considerable energy keeping the Mongolians out of China. For a brief period in the thirteenth century the Mongolians ruled China, but for much of the time they have been a minority group. All that is history. The area is largely desert land, but the great Yellow River runs through it and this yields, amongst other things, enormous quantities of scallops.

1 lb (450 g) prepared scallops
2 tablespoons soy or light vegetable oil
2–4 cloves garlic, peeled and finely chopped
2 teaspoons sesame seeds
2 inch (5 cm) cube fresh ginger, peeled and finely chopped
2 oz (50 g) onion, peeled and finely chopped

½ pint (300 ml) stock (any type) or water with a chicken stock cube
1 tablespoon hoisin sauce
1 tablespoon tomato ketchup
1 tablespoon light soy sauce
salt to taste
fresh coriander leaves for garnish

1. Wash and dry the scallops. Heat the oil in a wok or frying pan and stir-fry the garlic, sesame seeds, ginger and onion for 2 minutes.

2. Add the stock and bring to the simmer. Add the scallops and simmer for 5 minutes.

3. Add the hoisin sauce, tomato ketchup, soy sauce and salt to taste if needed.

4. It is ready to serve when it returns to the simmer. Garnish with fresh coriander.

STIR-FRIED CRAB AND EGG

Serves 4

In China they would use sand (or green) crabs, which are smallish and full of flavour, for this dish. There are many different species of crab and the better fishmonger will help you obtain something of quality. The idea of combining crab with scrambled egg originated in China at the turn of the century.

4 small cooked crabs, each weighing about 1 lb (450 g) with shell on
2 tablespoons sesame oil
2–4 cloves garlic, peeled and shredded
1½ inch (3.75 cm) cube fresh ginger, peeled and shredded
1 tablespoon red pepper in small strips
4–6 spring onions and their leaves, chopped

½ teaspoon turmeric
2 eggs
1 teaspoon five-spice powder
salt to taste

Garnish
finely chopped fresh parsley
mustard and cress

1. Crack open the crabs. Pull out all edible flesh keeping the pieces as chunky as you can.

2. Heat the oil in a wok or frying pan. Stir-fry the garlic, ginger, red pepper and spring onion for about 1 minute. Add the crab and stir-fry briskly until hot (remember it is already cooked). Add the turmeric to give a deep yellow colour.

3. Break in the eggs and carefully but continually stir-fry until almost set.

4. Sprinkle on the five-spice powder and add salt to taste.

5. Serve at once, garnished with parsley and mustard and cress.

STEAMED FISH IN THICK SAUCE

Serves 4

Carp is traditionally used in this dish. It is a particularly popular and abundant fish in China where they have several species including golden, silver, variegated (chub), rock and grass carp. Here we can use fresh water trout or salmon instead. This recipe originated in the Tang dynasty (618–907 AD).

2 whole trout or salmon each weighing 1–1¼ lb (450–560 g)

Sauce
2 tablespoons soy or light vegetable oil
1½ inch (3.75 cm) cube fresh ginger, peeled and thinly sliced
2 oz (50 g) pink onion, if available, or white onion, peeled and cut into rings
1 pint (600 ml) stock (any type)

2 oz (50 g) dried Chinese mushrooms, reconstituted (see page 146) and chopped
2 tablespoons yellow pepper in small diamonds
1 tablespoon cornflour
spicy salt to taste

Garnish
flaked almonds
finely chopped fresh parsley

1. Set up a large two-deck bamboo steamer over boiling water (see page 97).

2. Wash the fish but keep them whole.

3. Place one fish in each section of the steamer and steam for about 15 minutes.

4. During stage 3 heat the oil in a wok or frying pan. Stir-fry the ginger and onion for about 2 minutes.

5. Add the stock, mushrooms and yellow pepper and simmer for 5 minutes.

6. Mix the cornflour with enough water to make a thin paste.

7. Add the cornflour paste to the stock, stirring continuously until it stops thickening. Season to taste with spicy salt.

8. As soon as the fish are cooked to your liking, take them out of the steamer. Cut each fish in half and carefully remove the bones. Place the four halves on to a large flat serving dish.

9. Pour the sauce over the fish and garnish with flaked almonds and chopped parsley.

SZECHWAN FISH
WITH GROUND SPICY PORK

Serves 4

This remarkable combination of steamed fish with stir-fried ground or finely minced pork and ham is a traditional, colourful, aromatic and spicy dish. Chillies, ginger and shiu-fu (pickled herb mustard, but you can use mustard powder instead) are the spices. The dish is blended with a delightful red sauce just prior to serving.

4 pomfret or smoked haddock, with a
   total weight of about $1\frac{1}{2}$ lb (675 g)

Sauce
soy or sesame oil
1 inch (2.5 cm) cube fresh ginger,
   peeled and shredded
2 oz (50 g) pink or white onion, peeled
   and shredded
3 oz (75 g) pork, minced
1 oz (25 g) ham, minced
2 tablespoons Chinese red vinegar
1 tablespoon red bean paste
1 tablespoon dark soy sauce

2 oz (50 g) beetroot, minced
1–2 teaspoons shredded red chillies
1 teaspoon shiu-fu or $\frac{1}{2}$ teaspoon
   mustard powder
$\frac{1}{2}$ teaspoon ground Szechwan pepper
2–3 tablespoons stock (any type) or
   water
spicy salt to taste

Garnish
fried cashew nuts (see page 53)
finely chopped fresh coriander or
   parsley

1. Set up a double bamboo steamer over boiling water (see page 97).

2. Wash the fish and halve them. Place them in the steamer trays and steam for about 15 minutes.

3. During stage 2 heat the oil in a wok or frying pan. Stir-fry the ginger and onions for about 2 minutes. Add the pork and ham and stir-fry for 5 minutes, making sure that the mixture doesn't stick to the bottom.

4. Add the red vinegar, red bean paste, dark soy sauce, beetroot, chillies, shiu-fu and Szechwan pepper. Mix well and add enough stock or water to make the mixture flow easily but not so that it is too runny. Bring to the simmer. Season to taste with spicy salt.

5. Remove the fish from the steamer at the end of stage 2 (and when you are satisfied that it is properly cooked). Skin and fillet it. Cut it into bite-sized chunks and place them in a serving bowl.

6. Pour the sauce over the chunks, garnish with the cashew nuts and chopped herbs and serve.

FIVE-WILLOW FISH

Serves 4

There is a traditional Chinese story of a hermit who lived by a lake around which grew five willow trees. The hermit was a poet and a thinker and every day he would sit under one of his willows, dreaming. His favourite meal was a fresh fish straight from his lake. This dish symbolises the legend by garnishing each fish with five shredded vegetables of contrasting colours to represent the willow trees.

4 whole flat white fish fillets, such as plaice, each weighing about 6–8 oz (175–225 g)

Sauce
2 tablepoons sesame or light vegetable oil
2 cloves garlic, peeled and shredded
4–6 spring onions, chopped
1 tablespoon finely chopped pickled ginger
$\frac{1}{2}$ pint (300 ml) any type of stock or water

1 tablespoon potato flour
spicy salt to taste

Garnish
2 oz (50 g) Chinese radish (mooli)
2 oz (50 g) black mushrooms
2 oz (50 g) red peppers
2 oz (50 g) green peppers
2 oz (50 g) carrot

each of the garnish ingredients very finely shredded into 2 inch (5 cm) lengths

1. Set up a triple deck bamboo steamer over boiling water (see page 97).

2. Wash the fish fillets then place two into each of the bottom steamer trays.

3. Place the shredded garnish vegetables into the top steamer tray. Steam the fish and vegetables for 10 minutes.

4. During stage 3, heat the oil in a wok or frying-pan. Stir-fry the garlic and spring onion for 2 minutes. Add the pickled ginger and the stock or water and bring to the simmer.

5. Mix the potato flour with a little water and add it to the sauce to thicken it. Stir in until it is well mixed. Season to taste with spicy salt.

6. Keep on a low simmer until the fish and vegetables are cooked.

7. Remove the fish fillets from the steamer trays and place on a large flat serving dish. Pour over the sauce.

8. Place a little of each of the five steamed vegetables decoratively on top of or alongside each fish fillet. Serve promptly.

CHAPTER 9

VEGETABLES

There are a good number of vegetables in China. It may come as a surprise to realize that there are a good number of Chinese vegetarians too. Whether the vegetables are being cooked for vegetarian or non-vegetarian diners, the Chinese do not cook the vegetables on their own as we do. They add seasonings and sauces and they enjoy putting several vegetables together to make interesting combinations. Non-vegetarians add meat, poultry and/or seafood to their vegetables. I have had to take a simplified course in this chapter by, for the most part, omitting combinations. It is important to stress that you should feel totally free to add any other ingredients to any of these recipes if the mood takes you (it is impractical to keep saying this in each recipe). If you prefer, of course, each recipe is quite self-sufficient as it is.

I have concentrated mostly on Chinese special vegetables in this chapter. These include beansprouts, bamboo shoots, water chestnuts, Chinese cabbage, Chinese mushrooms, baby sweetcorn, mangetout, bean curd and lotus root. I also include a recipe using lotus nuts, which, although not specifically a vegetable, are used in a similar way by the Chinese. I have given a detailed description of each vegetable along with a sample recipe or two.

Vegetables which are common to China and the West such as peas, green beans, broad beans, carrots, courgettes, aubergines, broccoli, cucumber, celery, peppers, tomatoes and spinach need no introduction and each vegetable can be used in any way you wish, so I give just a few sample recipes to start you off.

Potatoes do not feature greatly in Chinese cooking. Originally from the New World they did not reach isolated China until the mid eighteenth century.

Beansprouts

Beansprouts (or bean-shoots) are an important Chinese vegetable. They are added to many dishes or may simply be steamed and served as an accompaniment. They are also one of nature's wonders. More or less any dried bean or lentil will sprout when water is applied under the correct conditions. The Chinese commonly use soya beans. The type readily available at our greengrocers are actually green moong bean sprouts.

Bamboo shoots

Bamboo shoots grow prolifically in China alongside all the main rivers. It is the tender, cone-shaped top part of the shoot which is eaten. These can be obtained fresh in the West from time to time but you are more likely to be served canned bamboo shoots in your local Chinese restaurant. These come in two forms – whole shoot tips or sliced. Fresh give the better flavour of course.

Water chestnuts

There are two types of water chestnuts which grow in Asia – the main type is called *pi-tsi*. It is an aquatic tuber of crunchy crisp texture, which bears no resemblance to our sweet chestnut so beloved at Christmas time. The Chinese water chestnut is normally only available canned in the West.

Chinese cabbage

There are many different types of cabbage used extensively in Chinese cooking and two are readily available in the West. Chinese leaves or pe-tsai (*Brassica pekinensis*) are long, firm and lettuce-like. The leaves can vary from pale to dark green. Both the stem and the leaves can be eaten. Pak-choi (*Brassica chinensis*) resembles chard, having dark green leaves and white edible stalks. A variety of pak-choi is Chinese flowering cabbage, choy-sum or gai-lan (*Brassica rapa*). This is eaten when young complete with its yellow flowers.

Baby sweetcorn

These are miniature sweetcorn cobs about 2–3 inches (5–7.5 cm) in length. Until recently they were only available canned. Now specially grown miniature fresh cobs are readily available in supermarkets everywhere.

Snow peas or mangetout

Also called sugar peas, these are flat, bright green young pea pods containing miniature peas. The entire pod is eaten and the only preparation required is washing and removing the little stalk. They require only brief cooking – steaming, blanching or stir-frying. Stir-frying enhances and retains their colour.

Mangetout grow on thin vines, the leaves of which are also eaten by the Chinese. They are occasionally available from London's Chinatown.

Chinese mushrooms

There are many species of Chinese mushroom. They grow in all areas of China and mainly in the rainy season. For as long as can be remembered the Chinese have preserved their mushrooms by drying them in the sun. They then keep more or less indefinitely. To reconstitute place in a large bowl and pour in enough boiling water to fill the bowl. Leave to soak for 30 minutes then drain. They give a distinctive flavour, colour and texture to Chinese cooking. I list the principal types below.

Dried black or brown mushrooms (*dong-gu*) have a thick cap and strongish fragrance. The larger ones with a pale colour and cracked skins have the best flavour.

Cloud ears or wood ears (*mu-er*) grow on trees and are used mainly for texture. They are brown and have a curly-leaf shape.

Silver fungus, snow ear or white wood fungus are similar to cloud or wood ears and whitish in colour. They are crunchy and pretty but rare, so are extremely expensive. They are available dried or canned.

Straw mushrooms are small and tear-drop shaped. They are very flavourful but are rarely available in the West in any form other than canned.

Other types occasionally available over here are **golden needle mushrooms** and the enormous **Hunan umbrella mushrooms**.

Tofu or bean curd

Better known by its Cantonese name, *doufu* or tofu, this has the texture of cheese. It can be either soft or firm, depending on the process. Normally it is white, but a red version is also available.

Tofu is made by soaking and puréeing white soya beans. The purée is then boiled in water which is strained to make soya milk. This is brought back to the simmer and a curdling agent, such as lemon juice, is added. It is then re-strained and the solid matter is compressed in moulds. After some time the result is a firm block of tofu. The process was first invented around 2,000 years ago by the scientists of an emperor of the Han dynasty (206 BC to 221 AD).

Tofu is easily obtained in packets from delicatessens and health-food shops. It is virtually flavourless and very high in protein. It is used for its texture and can be diced, sliced, minced or mashed then boiled, baked, stir-fried or deep-fried.

DEEP-FRIED TOFU

Serves 4

This is a favourite way of preparing bean curd. It can be served in a bowl on its own, or, more usually, it is added to another recipe. Try adding it to fried rice, chop suey or a wet dish such as Eastern China Braised Duck.

12 oz (350 g) block compressed tofu

To serve
spicy salt to taste
mustard and cress to garnish

1. Heat the deep-fryer to 375°F/190°C (chip-frying temperature).

2. Cut the tofu into cubes about $\frac{1}{2}$ inch (1.25 cm) square.

3. One after another place the cubes into the hot oil. Do this in two batches to prevent overloading the fryer and lowering the temperature.

4. Fry each batch for about 6–8 minutes. Remove from the deep-fryer and shake off excess oil. Stand on absorbent kitchen paper for a short while. Keep the first batch warm while frying the second batch.

5. If serving on its own, sprinkle with spicy salt to taste, garnish with mustard and cress and serve promptly.

BEAN CURD WITH PLUM SAUCE AND VEGETABLES

Serves 4

This is a good main course dish for a vegetarian. It contains a good balance of yin-yang textures, colours and tastes.

8 oz (225 g) block white or red
  compressed tofu
2–3 courgettes
8 oz (225 g) canned bamboo shoot tips
  or slices
2 tablespoons soy or light vegetable
  oil

2 oz (50 g) onion, peeled and finely
  chopped
3 tablespoons plum sauce
$\frac{1}{2}$ red pepper, cut into small diamonds
spicy salt to taste
sugar to taste

1. Cut the tofu into $\frac{3}{4}$ inch (2 cm) cubes.

2. Cut the courgettes and bamboo shoots into $\frac{3}{4}$ inch (2 cm) cubes. Any spare pieces can be added to the stock pot.

3. Heat the oil in a wok or frying pan. Stir-fry the onion for 20 seconds. Add the plum sauce and enough water to keep things just fluid.

4. When it is simmering add the courgettes and the red pepper and stir-fry for 2–3 minutes. Then add the bamboo shoots and the tofu and stir-fry for a couple more minutes.

5. Add spicy salt and sugar to taste and serve at once.

PAK-CHOI IN OYSTER SAUCE

Serves 4

This combination works very well, both in colour, taste and texture.

8 oz (225 g) pak-choi
1 tablespoon soy or light vegetable oil
2 cloves garlic, peeled and shredded
2 oz (50 g) onion, peeled and finely
  chopped

6 fl oz (175 ml) any type of stock or
  water
2 tablespoons oyster sauce
salt to taste

1. Wash the pak-choi thoroughly then chop it up, including the leaves and as much of the white stems as are tender enough.

2. Heat the oil in a wok or frying pan. Stir-fry the garlic and onion for 2 minutes.

3. Add the stock or water and when it starts to simmer add the pak-choi and the oyster sauce.

4. Mix well and bring back to the simmer. Add salt to taste and cook for 2–3 minutes. Serve promptly.

PE-TSAI WITH GINGER AND NUTS

Serves 4

Chinese white cabbage or leaves (known as pe-tsai) has little flavour of its own, but it picks up the flavourings around it and has an excellent crunchy texture provided that it is only lightly cooked.

8 oz (225 g) pe-tsai (Chinese leaves)
1 tablespoon soy or light vegetable oil
2 tablespoons finely chopped pickled ginger

4–5 spring onions, finely chopped
spicy salt to taste
about 40 Fried Cashew Nuts (see page 53)

1. Wash and chop the pe-tsai, using as much of the white stalks as you can.

2. Boil about 2 pints (1.2 litres) of water and blanch the cabbage for one minute. Drain.

3. During stage 2, heat the oil in a wok or frying pan. Stir-fry the pickled ginger for 30 seconds. Add the onion and stir-fry for 2 more minutes.

4. Add the cabbage and stir-fry briskly for about a minute. Season to taste with spicy salt.

5. Add the cashews and when hot it is ready to serve.

MUSHROOM WITH WALNUT

Serves 4

You can use any fresh or dry Chinese mushroom in this recipe, although cloud ears go particularly well, being rather similar in appearance to the nuts. It is the taste contrast between the mushrooms and nuts which makes this dish particularly good.

8 oz (225 g) dry cloud ear mushrooms
6 fl oz (175 ml) stock (any type) or
  water
2 tablespoons tomato ketchup
1 tablespoon light soy sauce

1 teaspoon hoisin sauce
4 oz (110 g) shelled walnuts
spicy salt to taste
fresh coriander leaves or parsley for
  garnish

1. Soak the dry mushrooms in ample boiling water for about half an hour to reconstitute them. Drain.

2. Discard the hard stalks and cut the mushrooms into small bite-sized pieces.

3. Heat the stock in a wok or pan. Add the tomato ketchup, soy sauce and hoisin sauce. When it is simmering, add the mushrooms.

4. Stir-fry until it is hot right through then add the walnuts and spicy salt to taste. Garnish with the coriander or parsley and serve immediately.

STUFFED BLACK MUSHROOMS

Serves 4

This recipe requires large black dried mushrooms. These are reconstituted and cooked then stuffed with a contrasting white sauce and garnished with colourful vegetables. The result is simply gorgeous and ideal for entertaining, especially as stages 1 to 5 can be completed well in advance.

12 dried black mushrooms, each about 3 inches (7.5 cm) in diameter
1 tablespoon sesame oil
2 cloves garlic, peeled and finely chopped
$\frac{1}{2}$ inch (1.25 cm) cube fresh ginger, peeled and finely chopped
$\frac{1}{2}$ teaspoon five-spice powder
$\frac{1}{2}$ teaspoon sesame seeds

$\frac{1}{2}$ oz (14 g) beansprouts, finely chopped
1 oz (25 g) cooked carrot, finely chopped
4 duck or hen's eggs

Garnish
tiny pieces of carrot and green peppers cut decoratively

1. Soak the mushrooms in boiling water for about half an hour to reconstitute them. Drain.

2. Discard the hard stalks then gently squeeze any extra water out of the mushrooms. Set aside on absorbent kitchen paper to dry further.

3. Heat the oil in a wok or frying pan. Stir-fry the garlic and ginger for 20 seconds. Add the five-spice powder, sesame seeds, beansprouts and carrot.

4. Separate the whites of 2 eggs and set aside. Beat together the 2 egg yolks and remaining 2 eggs then add to the wok and scramble so that the mixture is still quite runny. Remove the wok from the heat.

5. Spoon some egg and vegetable mixture into each of the mushrooms. Press it down into the cap to leave a rim and a concave depression in each mushroom.

6. To finish, set up a triple deck bamboo steamer over boiling water (see page 97).

7. Carefully spoon some egg white into the depression in each mushroom. Divide the mushrooms amongst the steamer trays, cover and steam until the egg white sets.

8. Place a little of the garnish vegetables on top of each mushroom and steam for a little while longer. Serve promptly.

FOUR-COLOURED BALL VEGETABLES

Serves 4

This is an attractive dish which differs in appearance from most other Chinese dishes. The effect is gained by using brown straw mushrooms, rather rounded and brown, pale green marrow, orange carrot and white water chestnuts. All these are brought together in an attractive pinkish sauce.

3 or 4 large carrots
1 medium-sized marrow
7 oz (200 g) straw mushrooms, fresh
   or canned
7 oz (200 g) water chestnuts, fresh or
   canned
2 tablespoons soy or light vegetable
   oil
2–4 cloves of garlic, peeled and sliced
2 inch (5 cm) cube fresh ginger, sliced

4–6 spring onions, chopped
$\frac{1}{2}$ pint (300 ml) stock (any type) or
   water
2 teaspoons tomato purée
2 tablespoons Chinese red vinegar
1 tablespoon light soy sauce
1 tablespoon red bean paste
2 tablespoons Chinese yellow rice
   wine or sweet sherry
spicy salt to taste

1. Prepare the carrots by hand paring them into balls about $\frac{3}{4}$ inch (2 cm) in diameter. Make about 16 balls.

2. Using a melon scooper make 16 balls out of the marrow. Any spare pieces of carrot and marrow can be used up in the stock pot.

3. Unless you are fortunate enough to have fresh straw mushrooms and water chestnuts, you'll have to open cans. Drain and add the liquid to the stock pot.

4. Heat the oil in a wok or frying pan. Stir-fry the garlic for 20 seconds. Add the ginger and spring onions and continue for 2 minutes.

5. Add $\frac{1}{2}$ pint (300 ml) stock, the tomato purée, carrot balls, vinegar, soy sauce and red bean paste. Bring to the simmer and simmer for about 5 minutes.

6. Add the marrow balls, mushrooms and chestnuts. Bring back to the simmer for about 2 more minutes.

7. Add the rice wine and spicy salt to taste. When hot it is ready to serve.

DRAGON'S TEETH

Serves 4

This enchantingly named vegetable dish is so called – according to the restaurant where I first encountered it in Sydney, Australia – because it is thought lucky to be in possession of a dragon's tooth. Baby sweetcorn cobs, carved Chinese snow radish (mooli) and white onion represent the teeth.

1 large mooli
½ Spanish onion
16 baby sweetcorn cobs, preferably
   fresh
1 tablespoon soy or light vegetable oil
1 inch (2.5 cm) cube fresh ginger,
   peeled and sliced

1–2 cloves garlic, peeled and sliced
6 fl oz (175ml) any type of stock or
   water
1 tablespoon yellow bean paste
spicy salt to taste
watercress leaves or strips of red
   pepper for garnish

1. Scrape the mooli then cut it into about 12 rectangles each about ½ inch (1.25 cm) wide by 2 inches (5 cm) long. Carve these into pointed curved teeth.

2. Cut the onion into 20 or so tooth-shaped triangles.

3. Blanch the sweetcorn cobs in boiling water for a couple of minutes.

4. Heat the oil in a wok or frying pan. Stir-fry the ginger and garlic for about 20 seconds.

5. Add the stock and the yellow bean paste and bring to the simmer.

6. Add the mooli, onion and sweetcorn and when simmering again season to taste with spicy salt. Transfer to a serving dish, garnish with watercress leaves or red pepper strips and serve.

SNOW PEA STIR-FRY

—— · ——

Serves 4

Snow peas are so light in flavour that their cooking must be equally light. Few dishes could be simpler than this one.

1 tablespoon soy or light vegetable oil   *spicy salt to taste*
3 fl oz (75 ml) vegetable stock or water   *sugar to taste*
8 oz (225 g) snow peas (mangetout)

1. Heat the oil in a wok or frying pan. Add the stock or water and, at once, the snow peas.

2. Stir-fry briskly for 2 minutes. Sprinkle with spicy salt and sugar to taste and serve at once.

Note: If you are ever lucky enough to get hold of the leaves, this is what you should do with them. Keep them on their stalks and steam them for 1 minute. Add to the Snow Pea Stir-fry at stage 2. Mix well and serve at once.

STIR-FRY CUCUMBER

—— · ——

Serves 4

The Chinese do not only eat raw cucumber. Here are two typical Chinese ways of cooking it.

1 large cucumber   *1 tablespoon light soy sauce*
1 tablespoon soy or light vegetable oil   *salt to taste*

1. Cut the cucumber into $\frac{1}{2}$ inch (1.25 cm) pieces.

2. Heat the oil in a wok or frying pan. Add the cucumber pieces and stir-fry briskly for 2 minutes.

3. Add the soy sauce and salt to taste. Serve promptly.

STUFFED CUCUMBER

Serves 4

This dish has a very attractive presentation but is very simple to prepare. The stuffing is minced spicy tofu.

2 large cucumbers
4 oz (110 g) mashed tofu
1–2 cloves garlic, peeled and finely
   minced
2–3 spring onions, finely chopped

1–2 fresh green chillies, finely
   chopped (optional)
$\frac{1}{2}$ teaspoon five-spice powder
$\frac{1}{4}$ teaspoon salt

1. Cut the top and bottom off the cucumber, cut out thin V-shapes in the skin down the length of each cucumber for better visual effect, then cut into 14 or 15 cylinders about 2 inches (5 cm) long. You will only need 3 cylinders per person but it is not a bad idea to have spares.

2. With a thin paring knife cut out the centre of each cylinder, leaving a wall at least $\frac{3}{16}$ inch (5 mm) thick.

3. Mix the mashed tofu with the garlic, spring onions, optional chillies, five-spice powder and salt.

4. Carefully fill the cylinders with the filling.

5. Set up a two-deck bamboo steamer over boiling water (see page 97).

6. Divide the stuffed cucumber cylinders between the steamer trays and steam for 3–4 minutes. Serve promptly.

SOUR PLUMS WITH CHERRY TOMATOES AND CELERY

Serves 4

Sour plums are a species of apricot and are normally bought in their dried form or in cans. They are pale in colour and very sour and should be used with sweeter ingredients to give a contrast.

4 oz (110 g) dried sour plums or 8 oz (225 g) canned sour plums, drained
1 tablespoon sesame or light vegetable oil
2 cloves garlic, peeled and finely chopped
2 tablespoons pickled ginger, chopped
3–4 spring onions, including leaves, chopped

1 tablespoon hoisin sauce
1 tablespoon plum sauce
6 fl oz (175 ml) stock (any type)
1 bunch celery, chopped into small pieces
8 oz (225 g) cherry tomatoes
spicy salt to taste
1 tablespoon finely chopped fresh parsley

1. Reconstitute the dried sour plums by soaking in ample cold water for 1 hour. Drain.

2. Heat the oil in a wok or frying pan. Stir-fry the garlic and pickled ginger for 30 seconds. Add the spring onions and continue stir-frying for a further 2 minutes.

3. Add the hoisin sauce, plum sauce, stock, plums and celery and simmer for 2 minutes.

4. Add the tomatoes and salt to taste.

5. When it returns to the simmer, add the parsley and serve promptly.

QUAIL'S EGGS AND LOTUS NUTS

Serves 4

The most commonly available eggs in China are duck eggs. Quail's eggs are also readily available and have the advantage of being most attractive in appearance.

Lotus nuts are normally available dried and must be soaked overnight in plenty of water during which time they double in size.

12 quail's eggs
1 tablespoon sesame or light vegetable
  oil
4–5 spring onions, chopped
1 iceburg lettuce, shredded
1 tablespoon soy sauce

4 tablespoons Chinese yellow rice
  wine or dry sherry
20 lotus nuts, soaked in water
  overnight (see above) and drained
spicy salt to taste
watercress to garnish

1. Put the quail's eggs into boiling water and simmer for precisely 4 minutes. Remove from the pan and place under cold running water for a couple of minutes. Shell the eggs, rinse and place in cold water until stage 3.

2. Heat the oil in a wok or frying pan. Stir-fry the spring onions for 2 minutes.

3. Add the lettuce and stir-fry briskly for 1 minute. Add the soy sauce and wine, the eggs and the lotus nuts.

4. When simmering, season to taste with spicy salt then garnish with watercress and serve.

CHAPTER 10

NOODLES AND RICE

A Chinese meal should always be a balance of staple dishes (*fan*) with other dishes (*chai*, see page 12). The main staples in Chinese cooking are noodles and rice.

NOODLES

Noodles are quite simply long thin threads or ribbons of dough. They are available fresh, in which case they must be used within a few days of purchase. It is more common, however, to use packet noodles which have been dried so that the threads become brittle. These will store almost indefinitely.

Chinese noodle making goes back at least 2,000 years and probably many more. It is very similar to Italian pasta making (pasta means dough in Italian). Claim and counter claim flow back and forth as to who invented the technique. Was it the Italians or the Chinese? Marco Polo, the famous Venetian explorer, visited China in 1270 and was astonished to find noodles there. Prior to the development of the Silk Road by 500 BC it is unlikely that China's culinary achievements were known in the West. In all probability pasta and noodles were developed independently of each other.

Most noodles are now made in the factory, but over the centuries it was always done by hand. Sometimes it is still possible to see them being made by the traditional method. I witnessed one such demonstration at India's top Chinese restaurant, The Teahouse of the August Moon, in Delhi. The Chinese chef started with a football-sized lump of dough which he pulled and divided first into two strands, then four, then eight and so on, stretching the strands by pulling them. In next to no time he had hundreds of perfect noodle threads which were ready for cooking. The technique is, of course, much harder than he made it look. That particular chef told me it had taken him five years to perfect the technique. We ordinary mortals must stick to shop-bought packet – or better still, fresh – noodles. Alternatively try making silver pin noodles (see page 161), which is one type of noodle that can be made at home quite easily.

Many factory-produced egg noodles contain additional flavourings such as chicken, beef, vegetables etc. I find these tastes totally synthetic and unnecessary. I recommend that you use only plain noodles and cook in flavours yourself as required.

There are three main families of noodles in Chinese cooking – egg, cellophane and rice – and I give basic cooking instructions for each. The cooking times for fresh and dried noodles are the same. You can use noodles literally with any other ingredient and to the limit of your imagination, so other recipes in this chapter are just a few examples to give you some ideas. Allow about 2 oz (50 g) dried noodles per person for a substantial helping.

Egg noodles

Egg noodles (*dan-mien*) are made from wheatflour, water and eggs (normally duck eggs). The threads vary considerably in width from very thin strands to ribbons about $\frac{1}{3}$ inch (8 mm) wide. They also vary in colour from pale cream to deep yellow, depending on how many eggs are used. Factories use egg powder and food colouring to achieve the effect.

Follow the cooking instructions and quantities on the packet. As a general rule dried egg noodles cook fast, as they have actually been pre-cooked.

1. Bring plenty of water to the boil in a large pan.

2. Immerse the noodles in the water and when it returns to the boil, take the pan off the heat, cover and leave the noodles in the water for 5–8 minutes or according to packet instructions.

3. Strain and proceed with your chosen recipe.

Wheat noodles

Wheat noodles (*mie* or *mien*) are less common but used from time to time in Chinese cookery. They are made from wheat flour and water and are formed into flat sticks or ribbons of varying widths. Cook as for egg noodles (above).

Cellophane noodles

Cellophane noodles (*fun-sie*) or bean thread noodles are made from the thick paste (or dough) of the green soya bean or moong-bean. Generally these noodles are very small in diameter and they are translucent, hence their name. Their main use is in soups and stews, or deep fried as a garnish.

Cooking instructions are usually given on the packet. Normally all that is required is to soak the dried noodles in hot water for between 5 and 8 minutes (see egg noodles, above). Alternatively they can be deep-fried. Be careful not to overload the pan as they will whoosh up at first and then settle down after about 10 seconds. Remove from the oil after about 30 seconds.

Rice noodles

Rice noodles (*ho-fun*) are made from a rice-flour dough and they are always bright white in colouring. They come in three basic forms. The first is straight flat ribbons ranging from $\frac{1}{16}$ (1 mm) to $\frac{1}{4}$ (4 mm) in thickness, called rice sticks (or *hofun*). Thicker rice sticks are called *kway teow*. The third variety is curly noodles, known as rice vermicelli (*mie-fun* or *mie hoon*).

Follow the cooking instructions and quantities on the packet. Cooking generally entails soaking the noodles in hot water for between 10 and 15 minutes, depending on the thickness of the noodles. Rice noodles can also be deep-fried (see cellophane noodles above).

Opposite THE SHANGHAI DINNER PARTY
Clockwise from the top: Fire Pot containing stock and dried chrysanthemums with raw ingredients (page 70, note the wire ladles used for cooking), Stuffed Chinese Pears (page 173), Fortune Cookies (page 178), Stir-fried Crab and Egg (page 140), Yangtze Rabbit (page 133), Stir-Fry Cucumber with spring onion tassel garnish (pages 31 and 154) and Thin Pastry Crisps (page 51).

Facing page 161 PEKINESE IMPERIAL BANQUET
Clockwise from the top: Peking Phoenix Emperor Prawns (page 135), Four Coloured Ball Vegetables (page 152), Pancakes in a bamboo steamer (page 121), Peking Duck with spring onions and cucumber (page 119), Hoisin Sauce (page 40), Plum Sauce (pages 40–41), Barbecued Pork (page 115), Chilli and Garlic Sauce (page 42), The Chicken and The Egg (page 72), and Eight Treasure Fried Rice (page 168).

SILVER PIN NOODLES WITH BEANSPROUTS

Serves 4

The silver pin or silver needle noodle is one form of Chinese noodle that you can easily make at home. A cornflour and wheat flour dough is hand rolled into short needles with pointed ends. They should resemble beansprouts in colour, shape and size.

Noodles
4 oz (110 g) plain white flour
2 tablespoons cornflour
water

Sauce
1 tablespoon soy or light vegetable oil
4 spring onions, finely chopped
1 teaspoon white sugar
1 tablespoon light soy sauce

1 tablespoon Chinese yellow rice wine
  or dry sherry
3 fl oz (75 ml) any type of stock
2 tablespoons frozen peas, thawed
2 tablespoons frozen shrimps, thawed
  (optional)
4 tablespoons beansprouts
salt to taste

Noodles

1. Mix the flours together in a large mixing bowl. Add enough water to make a firm pliable dough. Knead until smooth then leave to stand for about 10 minutes.

2. Knead the dough once more then divide it into several pieces.

3. Take one piece and roll it into a long sausage. Cut this into short sausages and roll each into thin, pointed needles about the size of a beansprout.

4. Set up a double-deck bamboo steamer over boiling water (see page 97).

5. Divide the noodles between the steamer trays and steam for 3–4 minutes.

Sauce

6. During stage 5, heat the oil in a wok or frying pan. Stir-fry the spring onions for one minute.

7. Add the sugar, soy sauce and wine or sherry. When sizzling, add the stock, peas, optional shrimps and the beansprouts. When everything is hot, add the steamed noodles and salt to taste. Serve when sizzling.

BLACK BEAN NOODLES

Serves 4

This is a typical stir-fry noodle dish incorporating colourful peppers and Chinese leaves. Use the type of noodle of your choice.

8 oz (225 g) noodles, any type
2 tablespoons soy or light vegetable oil
2 cloves garlic, peeled and shredded
1 inch (2.5 cm) cube fresh ginger, peeled and sliced
4 spring onions, chopped
1 tablespoon green pepper cut into diamond shapes

1 tablespoon red pepper cut into diamond shapes
2 oz (50 g) pe-tsai (Chinese leaves), coarsely shredded
1 tablespoon black beans, canned or fresh
1 tablespoon dark soy sauce
spicy salt to taste

1. Steam or boil the noodles (see pages 159–60).

2. Heat the oil in a wok or frying pan. Stir-fry the garlic and ginger for 20 seconds. Add the spring onions and continue stir-frying for a further minute.

3. Add the pepper diamonds, Chinese leaves, black beans and soy sauce. Stir-fry briskly until sizzling.

4. Add the strained freshly-cooked noodles and salt to taste. Stir until hot then serve.

CRISPY BEEF NOODLES

Serves 4

This recipe makes the most of deep-fried noodles. Again any type of noodle can be used. Crispy noodles can be served by crumbling them over the meal. Alternatively crispy noodles can be the major ingredient in a stir-fry dish such as this recipe.

10 oz (300g) noodles, any type
2 tablespoons soy or light vegetable oil
2–4 cloves garlic, peeled and finely chopped

4 spring onions, chopped
8 oz (225 g) trimmed fillet steak, shredded
2 oz (50 g) frozen green beans, thawed
1 tablespoon dark soy sauce

1. Heat the deep-fryer to 375°F/190°C (chip-frying temperature).

2. Break up the noodles into three or four batches.

3. Place one batch into the hot oil. It will whoosh up fairly fast then settle down. Remove from the oil after about 30 seconds, shaking to remove excess oil.

4. Repeat stage 3 with the remaining batches of noodles.

5. Put the crispy noodles into a serving bowl and place in a warmer or low oven.

6. Heat the oil in a wok or frying-pan. Stir-fry the garlic for 20 seconds. Add the spring onions and continue stir-frying for a further minute.

7. Add the shredded steak and stir-fry for another 3–4 minutes.

8. Add the beans and soy sauce, and bring to a sizzle. Pour the sauce over the noodles just prior to serving. Serve promptly otherwise the noodles will go soggy.

SEA-SPICY NOODLE BALLS

Serves 4

In this unusual form the noodles of your choice are mixed with a purée of prawns and rolled into small balls which are then deep-fried. They can then be served as they are or added to a sauce.

5 oz (150 g) noodles
8 oz (225 g) cornflour
4 oz (110 g) peeled prawns, mashed
  or puréed

2 teaspoons ten-spice powder
1 tablespoon chopped fresh coriander
  leaves
mustard and cress for garnish

1. Steam or boil the noodles (see pages 159–60).

2. Strain the noodles and leave until cool enough to handle. Chop them finely.

3. Mix the cornflour with the prawns, ten-spice powder and coriander. Add enough water to make a batter of dropping consistency.

4. Add the chopped noodles and if necessary stiffen the mixture with a little more cornflour.

5. Heat the deep-fryer to 375°F/190°C (chip-frying temperature).

6. Place a dollop of the mixture on a floured work surface and roll it into a ball about $\frac{3}{4}$ inch (2 cm) in diameter.

7. Repeat with the remaining mixture. Divide the balls into two batches.

8. Cook the first batch by lowering the balls, one by one, into the hot oil. Deep-fry until golden and cooked through (about 8 minutes).

9. Remove the balls from the deep-fryer and shake off excess oil. Transfer to a warmer or low oven.

10. Repeat stages 8 and 9 with the second batch of balls.

11. Serve as they are garnished with mustard and cress, or add them to a sauce.

RICE

Most restaurants turn out a rice which is fairly fluffy and this is the way most of us seem to prefer it. However it is quite acceptable for Chinese rice to be slightly glutinous. Indeed some species of Chinese rice will only cook that way no matter what you do, and glutinous and sticky is the way many Chinese prefer their rice, especially in the north and west of China. One advantage of this type of rice is that it's much easier to pick up with chopsticks.

With this in mind it is quite clear that there is a great deal more flexibility in rice cooking in China than there is in India, where it is essential to achieve separate fluffy grains.

The recipe below will produce fluffy rice. The secret lies in using the best available rice and in accurate cooking time and in allowing the rice to rest after cooking. For example Indian long-grained basmati rice produces very aromatic fluffy rice if cooked for about 8–10 minutes and then allowed to rest and dry out in a low oven for at least 30 minutes.

If you want slightly stickier rice, cook for slightly longer or use Patna or short-grained rice. If you want *very* sticky rice, buy Thai or Japanese glutinous rice and cook it for about 15 minutes.

Rice can be frozen and reheated perfectly well but it takes so little time to cook and flavour that I prefer to cook it fresh each time.

Flavoured rice not only looks very attractive but tastes good too. On pages 166–8 are five popular restaurant flavourings for rice. Simply boil the rice as described below, then cook in your chosen flavouring. Peas and/or sweetcorn can be added for extra colour.

PLAIN RICE

Serves 4

8–12 oz (225–350 g) basmati rice
2–3 pints (1.2–1.8 litres) water

1. Pick through the rice to remove grit and impurities.

2. Boil the water. It is not necessary to salt it.

3. While it is heating up, rinse the rice briskly with fresh cold water until most of the starch is washed out. Run hot tap water through the rice at the final rinse. This minimises the temperature reduction of the boiling water when you put the rice into it.

4. When the water is boiling properly, put the rice into the pan. Start timing. Put the lid on the pan until the water comes back to the boil, then remove. It takes 8–10 minutes from the start. Stir frequently.

5. After about 6 minutes, taste a few grains. As soon as the centre is no longer brittle but still has a good *al dente* bite to it, drain off the water. The rice should seem slightly *under*cooked.

6. Shake off all excess water, then place the strainer on to a dry tea towel which will help remove the last of the water.

7. After a minute place the rice in a warmed serving dish. You can serve it now or, preferably, put it into a very low oven or warming drawer for at least $\frac{1}{2}$ hour. As it dries, the grains will separate and become fluffy. It can be held in the warmer for several hours if needed.

EGG FRIED RICE

Serves 4

The strips of yellow egg contrast attractively with the white of the rice.

1 tablespoon soy or light vegetable oil
1 egg, beaten

cooked rice (about 8–12 oz/225–350 g uncooked weight)
spicy salt to taste

1. Heat the oil in a flat frying pan.

2. Pour in the beaten egg, spreading it thinly around the bottom of the pan. Cook as for an omelette.

3. When cooked, remove from the pan, allow to cool a little then cut it into thin strips.

4. Put the rice into the hot frying pan (or a wok) and stir-fry until it is hot. Add the egg strips and season to taste with spicy salt.

SHRIMP FRIED RICE

Serves 4

This is a very popular restaurant variation of fried rice. The pink and white look pretty too.

1 tablespoon soy or light vegetable oil
20–30 small shrimps, peeled and
  thawed

cooked rice (about 8–12 oz/225–
  350 g uncooked weight)
spicy salt to taste

1. Heat the oil in a wok or frying pan.

2. Add the shrimps and stir-fry briskly for 2–3 minutes.

3. Add the rice and stir-fry until it is hot. Season to taste with spicy salt.

CHICKEN FRIED RICE

Serves 4

This recipe is a good way of using up leftover cooked chicken. You could alternatively use crispy duck, Barbecued Pork or ham instead of the chicken.

2 oz (50 g) cooked chicken breast meat
1 tablespoon soy or light vegetable oil

cooked rice (about 8–12 oz/225–
  350 g uncooked weight)
spicy salt to taste

1. Chop the meat into small cubes about $\frac{1}{4}$ inch (6 mm) square.

2. Heat the oil in a wok or frying pan.

3. Add the cubes of meat and stir-fry briskly for about 1 minute.

4. Add the rice and stir-fry until it is hot. Season to taste with spicy salt.

VEGETABLE FRIED RICE

Serves 4

Use diced mixed frozen vegetables for the best colour and to save preparation time. Serve promptly or the green peas will turn a greyish colour.

1 tablespoon soy or light vegetable oil
2 oz (50 g) diced mixed vegetables,
thawed if frozen

cooked rice (about 8–12 oz/225–
350 g uncooked weight)
spicy salt to taste

1. Heat the oil in a wok or frying pan.

2. Add the vegetables and stir-fry briskly for 1 minute.

3. Add the rice and stir-fry until it is hot. Season to taste with spicy salt.

EIGHT TREASURE FRIED RICE

Serves 4

Eight is a Chinese lucky number so care should be taken to include eight flavouring ingredients in this rice. You can of course use less or more as the mood takes you, provided that you aren't superstitious. This makes a good dinner party rice.

1 tablespoon soy or light vegetable oil
2 oz (50 g) total weight of the eight
'treasures' of your choice chosen
from the following: omelette strips
(see page 166); cooked shrimps;
diced cooked chicken, duck, beef or
ham; cooked peas or sweetcorn

kernels; diced cooked carrots, green
beans, parsnips, or mushrooms;
diced cherries, tangerines, or other
fruit
cooked rice (about 8–12 oz/225–
350 g uncooked weight)
spicy salt to taste

1. Heat the oil in a wok or frying pan.

2. Add the 'treasures' and stir-fry briskly until they are hot.

3. Add the boiled rice and stir-fry until it is hot enough. Season to taste with spicy salt.

CHAPTER 11

DESSERTS AND COOKIES

The Chinese do not have a concept, as we do, of serving a starter, a main course and a pudding. They do believe in serving separate courses on formal occasions, particularly at banquets, but there is no laid down order of play.

Probably as a result of this there is a relatively small choice on the desserts menu of the Chinese restaurant. All too often one is confronted with fruit salad, canned lychees or ice-cream.

I have no objection to a good fruit salad and the recipe in this chapter makes an exceptionally delicious one, especially if served in the carved melon cup. Lychees, too, can be refreshing and interesting, if fresh rather than canned, and ice-cream is always a safe choice to end a Chinese meal. However there are other Chinese desserts that are worth the minimal amount of effort they take to make, and this chapter suggests some that you may be unfamiliar with.

The chapter concludes with one of China's surprise treats – the Fortune Cookie.

EIGHT TREASURE RICE PUDDING

Serves 4

Eight is a lucky number in China so if you want good luck you must be sure to include eight fruits and nuts in this rice pudding. It can be served hot or cold and is not unlike a Christmas or treacle pudding in final appearance.

12 oz (375 g) glutinous or other rice	*2 tablespoons dragon's eyes or*
1 slice pineapple	*sultanas*
2 peaches, skinned	*12 black seedless grapes, quartered*
1 large apple, skinned and cored	*$\frac{1}{2}$ teaspoon ground cassia bark or*
1 tangerine, peeled	*cinnamon*
12 maraschino cherries, quartered	*4 tablespoons brown sugar*
12 shelled walnuts, halved	*6 tablespoons clear honey*

1. Boil the rice for 20 minutes then drain. It will by now be quite sticky.

2. Whilst the rice is cooking, cut the pineapple, peaches, apple and tangerines into small bite-sized pieces (about $\frac{1}{4}$ inch/6 mm square).

3. Mix the rice with the fruit and nuts, cassia bark or cinnamon and sugar.

4. Rub a pudding basin with butter then press the rice mixture into it.

5. Set up a bamboo steamer over boiling water (see page 97).

6. Place the steamer tray upside down on the pudding bowl. Invert (so that the tray is now the right way up and the bowl upside down) and place the tray and bowl over the water.

7. Steam for 20 minutes. Towards the end of the steaming time heat the honey in a small pan.

8. Ease the pudding out of its bowl on to a serving plate.

9. Pour over the hot honey and serve very hot.

Note: The traditional way to prepare this dish is to arrange the fruit in a decorative and symmetrical pattern at the bottom of the pudding bowl, before pressing the rice in on top and steaming as above. When turned out, the effect is very pretty.

TOFFEE APPLES OR BANANAS

Serves 4

A spectacular and sumptuous dessert perfect for entertaining. It was developed, as you might expect, for the titilation of the Peking emperors. It is also known as Drawn Thread Apple, Candied Apple or Peking Glazed Apple. It is now the highlight of the Chinese restaurant pudding menu. Bite-sized chunks of apple or banana are coated in batter, deep-fried, then dipped into hot liquid toffee made from sugar, water and oil. They are then plunged briefly into iced water which makes the coating crisp and produces attractive threads of toffee. Practise the technique first before doing it for guests.

4 dessert apples or bananas

Batter
5 oz (150 g) plain flour
1 oz (25 g) cornflour
1 tablespoon soy or light vegetable oil
6 (175 ml) water

Toffee
6 fl oz (175 ml) water
2 tablespoons soy or light vegetable oil
6 oz (175 g) white sugar

1. Make the batter first by putting the flours into a large mixing bowl. Add the oil and enough water to make a pourable (but not thin) batter. Set aside.

2. Peel and core the apples or peel the bananas. Cut into bite-sized pieces.

3. Heat the deep-fryer to 375°F/190°C (chip-frying temperature).

4. Dip one piece of apple into the batter and drop it into the deep-fryer. Add the next piece and the next until the deep-fryer is full but not overloaded. Cook in two batches if necessary. Fry until golden and hot right through (about 6 minutes). Remove, drain and keep warm.

5. To make the toffee, bring the water to the boil, then add the oil and sugar. Continue to boil, stirring continuously until it thickens to the point where it runs off a spoon slowly.

6. Have ready a bowl of iced water. Just prior to serving dip one piece of warm cooked apple or banana into the hot toffee. At once dip it into the iced water. The toffee will immediately go crisp and will form threads. Serve immediately.

Note: It is fun to do stage 6 at the table, letting the diners dip their own apple or banana into the toffee (kept hot over a table stove) and the icy water using chopsticks.

LYCHEES

Serves 4

These are almost the standard Chinese restaurant cliché. Most restaurants serve canned lychees, and the resultant white fruit are rather disappointing. If you can obtain fresh lychees in their attractive red skins, serve them with this simple syrup enhanced with liqueur and nuts and you will have an excellent dessert.

1 lb (450 g) fresh lychees
2 tablespoons soy or light vegetable oil
8 fl oz (250 ml) water

6 oz (175 g) white sugar
2 fl oz (50 ml) Cointreau
2–3 tablespoons flaked almonds

1. Peel the lychees and discard the red skin. Quarter the lychees and discard the large pip.

2. Heat the oil and water in a wok or frying pan. When simmering add the sugar and stir until it dissolves and the liquid thickens a little.

3. Remove the wok from the heat and allow to cool.

4. Add the lychees and chill in the fridge until required.

5. Just prior to serving add the Cointreau and decorate with flaked almonds.

STUFFED CHINESE PEARS

Serves 4

For an authentic version of this Szechwan recipe one should use the Chinese snow pear – a soft sweet pear unobtainable in the West. However a soft round pear such as a Williams or Packham makes a very acceptable Western alternative.

4 tablespoons cold cooked rice	*4 soft ripe pears*
12–16 dragon's eyes or sultanas	*icing sugar for dusting*
2 teaspoons granulated sugar	*4 maraschino cherries*

1. Set up a bamboo steamer over boiling water (see page 97).

2. Mix together the rice, dragon's eyes or sultanas and sugar.

3. Peel the pears, cut off the tops and the bases. Remove the core.

4. Stuff down the core of each pear with the rice mixture.

5. Place the pears on the steamer tray, cover and steam for about 15–20 minutes.

6. Just prior to serving, dust with icing sugar and top each pear with a maraschino cherry.

SWEET WONTONS

Makes 16 wontons

Wontons are small pastries steamed or fried as already described on pages 91–9. When made with a sweet filling they become a delicious dessert. The filling here contains a mixture of nuts and fruit.

16 wonton wrappers (see pages 91–2)

Sweet filling
3 oz (75 g) chopped almonds   *1 oz (25 g) minced or crushed pineapple*
1 oz (25 g) chopped walnuts   *1 tablespoon honey*

1. Mix the filling ingredients together into a cohesive paste.

2. Put a teaspoon on to each wonton wrapper. Fold into the shape of your choice (see pages 94–6).

3. Deep-fry for 6–8 minutes, following the instructions on page 98.

FRUIT FRITTERS

Serves 4

This recipe owes little to authentic Chinese cooking and everything to the restaurateurs in Hong Kong. Based on a traditional Singaporean recipe, it is however a very tasty Chinese restaurant dessert. Here I use bananas, but there are many other suitable fruits including pineapple, lychees, strawberries, peaches and plums.

6 oz (175 g) plain flour
2 tablespoons sesame seeds

4 bananas
icing sugar for dusting

1. Put the flour and sesame seeds in a large mixing bowl. Add enough water to make a batter of pouring consistency.

2. Heat the deep-fryer to 375°F/190°C (chip-frying temperature).

3. Peel the bananas and cut into $1\frac{1}{2}$ inch (3.75 cm) segments.

4. Dip one piece of banana into the batter and place it in the deep-fryer.

5. Repeat stage 4 until the fryer is full but not overloaded. (You may need to cook the banana in two batches.) Cook until golden and cooked right through (about 8–10 minutes). Drain and keep warm.

6. Just prior to serving, dust with icing sugar and serve hot.

RED BEAN CURD SWEET PANCAKE

Makes 12–14 pancakes

This pancake is spread with a layer of sweet red tofu and laced with a honey syrup. Delicious!

Pancakes
4 oz (110 g) plain white flour
2 oz (50 g) butter, melted, plus extra
  for frying
2 eggs, beaten
½ pint (300 ml) milk, warmed
3–4 drops vanilla essence

Filling
8 oz (225 g) red tofu, mashed
1 tablespoon brown sugar

Syrup
3 oz (75 ml) golden syrup
3 oz (75 ml) honey
2 tablespoons lemon juice

1. To make the pancakes, sift the flour into a bowl and mix in the melted butter, eggs, warm milk and vanilla essence. Beat well and leave to stand for about 10 minutes. The batter should be of pouring consistency.

2. Mix the tofu and sugar together for the filling.

3. Melt a little butter in a very hot omelette or griddle pan. Pour in enough batter which when 'swirled' around the pan makes a thin pancake.

4. Cook until set, then turn over and briefly cook the other side. Turn the pancake out and place some of the filling across the centre of the pancake.

5. Fold in two sides then roll it up to create a cylinder. Keep warm while you cook and fill the other pancakes.

6. Heat the syrup ingredients. Pour over the pancakes and serve.

FRESH FRUIT SALAD IN MELON CUPS

Fresh fruit is always popular and nutritious. You can choose any fresh fruit that is in the market.

For that authentic touch you may like to put together a combination of fruits which originated in China. This might include apricots, bananas, cherries, kumquats, kiwi fruit (also called Chinese gooseberries), lychees, mandarines (tangerines), nectarines, oranges, peaches and plums. Simply cut into bite-sized cubes and sprinkle with sugar and sweet sherry to taste.

And for that really special occasion, chopped fruit can be served in decorated melon cups. After carving them, put them empty into the freezer half an hour before serving. Fill with the fruit salad just prior to serving. They then arrive frosty and 'steaming' at the table. The carved melon bowls are also an attractive way of serving soup.

You will need a small round green melon for each person.

1. Cut off the top third of each melon and reserve.

2. Carve patterns of your choice into the melons (dragon, phoenix, etc). You can either carve the image out of the skin (a negative image) or carve it in reverse, so the image is the skin and everything else is carved away (a positive image).

3. Next, very carefully cut the melon flesh away from the inside to create four bowls. The flesh can be added to the fruit salad.

4. Next make stands to support the melons. Cut a depression in the skin of each of the four melon tops. The melons should sit in the depressions without moving around.

5. Place the melon bowls in the freezer for about an hour prior to serving.

6. Just before serving remove from the freezer and fill with the fruit salad. Serve sitting on their melon bases.

FORTUNE COOKIES

Makes 24 cookies

Fortune cookies are small biscuits – in fact they are discs folded into a crescent shape whilst still warm. There is more to them than that, though. Inside each one is a paper fortune or good luck message, usually with a piece of proverbial wisdom. Easy to make and great fun to serve at the tea or coffee stage of the meal, they are ideal for entertaining and you can tailor your messages to suit the assembled company. I give a few suggestions for fortunes to start you off.

The story goes that it was Chinese conspirators back in the Ming dynasty (1368–1644) who transmitted secret messages to their various dissident factions by planting them inside small biscuits.

The idea was carried a step further during the nineteenth century when school teachers ensured that 'pearls of wisdom' in the form of learned quotations were found by their pupils inside folded biscuits.

Fortune cookies emerged in their present form early this century in the world's first 'Chinatown', that of San Francisco. The many restaurants were frequented by Chinese sailors and the good luck messages were designed to wish them well on their voyages.

8 oz (225 g) plain white flour	*6 tablespoons sesame or light*
3 tablespoons cornflour	*vegetable oil*
6 tablespoons granulated sugar	*3 egg whites, beaten*
4 drops vanilla essence	*butter for greasing*
pinch of salt	*24 folded messages*

1. Sift the flours into a large mixing bowl. Add the sugar, vanilla essense, salt and oil and enough water to make a stiff pourable batter.

2. Heat the oven to 325°F/160°C/Gas 3.

3. Grease two baking sheets.

4. Drop a tablespoon of batter on to one of the baking sheets and spread into a thin round disc about 3 inches (7.5 cm) in diameter. Repeat with the remaining batter, leaving space between the discs. You may have to cook them in two or more batches.

5. Bake for about 15 minutes or until golden. While still hot remove them one at a time from the baking sheet and place a folded message on top. Fold the discs in half then bend inwards to form the cresent shape. They will fold and bend whilst warm.

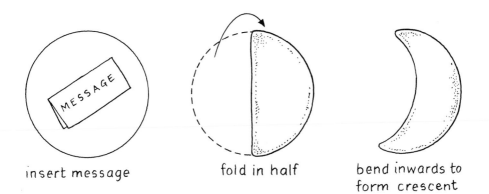

insert message   fold in half   bend inwards to form crescent

6. Place each one into a pattie or tart tin (which will prevent them from unfolding) and allow to cool completely.

7. Store in an airtight container until required.

Fortunes

Tomorrow is your lucky day. Put off today what you can do tomorrow.

Expect a message from a friend or loved one. Remember truth is stranger than fiction.

You may come into some wealth soon. Then you'll find out who your friends are.

It seems you are going to travel soon. Pack up your troubles and get going.

You are destined to be attracted to a tall, dark and handsome stranger.

Watch out for Wednesday next. Something unusual may happen.

Someone seeking your advice won't heed it, so withold it, and stay friends.

Stop looking over your shoulder – you'll crick your neck and bump into a lamp-post.

One good friend is worth 1000 acquaintances.

You have enjoyed a great meal. Thank the cook with showerings of gold.

ALMOND BISCUITS

Makes about 12 biscuits

These delightful little biscuits can be eaten at any time or after a meal with tea or coffee.

4 oz (110 g) butter
4 oz (110 g) caster sugar
1 egg

2 tablespoons ground almonds
3–4 drops vanilla essence
5 oz (150 g) plain white flour

1. Mix the butter and sugar together in a large mixing bowl, until pale and creamy.

2. Add the egg, ground almonds, vanilla essence and flour and work into a soft well-mixed dough.

3. Heat the oven to 375°F/190°C/Gas 5. Grease two baking sheets.

4. Divide the dough into 4, then divide each quarter into 5 (so that there are now 20 small lumps).

5. Roll one lump into a small ball then press it down on to one of the baking sheets. Repeat with the remaining lumps of dough, leaving space between the balls on the baking sheets.

6. Bake for 12 minutes, then inspect. They should be pale gold and crispy looking. If not bake for a little longer.

7. Allow to cool, then remove from the baking sheets and store in an air-tight container.

APPENDIX 1
— · —

The Curry Club

Pat Chapman has always had a deep-rooted interest in spicy food, curry in particular, and over the years he has built up a huge pool of information which he felt could be usefully passed on to others. He conceived the idea of forming an organization for this purpose.

Since it was founded in January 1982, The Curry Club has built up a membership of several thousands. It has a marchioness, some lords and ladies, a captain or two of industry, generals, admirals and air marshals (not to mention a sprinkling of ex-colonels), and it has celebrity names – actresses, politicians, rock stars and sportsmen. It has an airline (Air India), a former RN warship (HMS *Hermes*) and a hotel chain (the Taj group). It has members on every continent, including a good number of Asian members, but by and large the membership is a typical cross-section of the Great British Public, ranging in age from teenage to dotage, in occupation from refuse collectors to receivers, high street traders to high court judges, and tax inspectors to taxi drivers. There are students and pensioners, millionaires and unemployed ... thousands of people who have just one thing in common – a love of curry and spicy foods.

Members receive a bright and colourful magazine four times a year, which has regular features on curry and the curry lands. It includes news items, recipes, reports on restaurants, picture features and contributions from members and professionals alike. The information is largely concerned with curry but by popular demand it now includes regular input on other exotic and spicy cuisines such as those of the Middle East and China. The Club has produced a wide selection of publications, including the books listed on page 2, all published by Piatkus. There is also a cookery video.

Obtaining ingredients required for Indian, Oriental and Middle Eastern cooking can be difficult, but The Curry Club makes it easy with its well-established and efficient mail order service. Over 500 items are stocked, including spices, pickles, pastes, dry foods, tinned foods, gift items, publications and specialist kitchen and tableware.

On the social side, the Club organizes regular activities all over the UK. These range from monthly 'nights' in London and specific 'nights' elsewhere, enabling members to meet the Club organisers, discuss queries, buy supplies and enjoy spicy snacks or meals. The Club also holds day and residential weekend cookery courses, gourmet nights to selected restaurants, and similar enjoyable outings.

Top of the list is our regular Curry Club Gourmet Trip to India and other spicy countries. We take a small group of curry enthusiasts to the chosen country and tour the incredible sights, in between sampling the delicious foods of each region.

If you'd like to know more, write to **The Curry Club, PO Box 7, Haslemere, Surrey, GU27 1EP – Telephone: 0428 658327.**

APPENDIX 2

—— · ——

The Store Cupboard

Below are all the specialist non-perishable ingredients used in this book. Items marked * are used in three or fewer recipes.

This list may look formidable, but all the items will keep for a long time if stored correctly. They are best kept in airtight containers in a damp-free, cool place in the dark or out of direct sunlight. The items that are available by post from The Curry Club are those which state quantities (see Appendix 1 for address). The quantities are either metric or imperial depending on the manufacturer:

Spices and flavourers
*Beetroot powder   25 g
Cassia bark, whole   30 g
Cassia bark, ground   20 g
Chilli powder   100 g
Chilli, whole, dried   11 g
Chinese five-spice powder   25 g
Cinnamon, whole   20 g
Cinnamon, ground   25 g
Clove, whole   20 g
Clove, ground   25 g
Curry powder, mild, Chinese   25 g
Fennel seeds   25 g
Garlic powder   100 g
Liquorice powder
*MSG (monosodium glutamate)
*Mustard powder
*Prawn powder
*Red food colouring, chemical
Sea salt
Sesame seeds, white   50 g
Star anise   20 g
Szechwan peppercorns   20 g
*Turmeric   100 g

Dry foods
Cashew nuts
Cornflour
Custard powder
Mushroom: cloud ear
   dried black/brown   6 pieces
Noodles: cellophane bean thread   250 g
   egg   250 g
   rice sticks   400 g
   rice vermicelli   500 g
   wheat
Potato flour
*Prawn crackers   8 oz

Sauces
Chilli
Chilli and garlic   150 ml
Curry paste, mild   190 g
Hoisin   227 g
Oyster   200 g
Plum   227 g
Sesame paste (tahini)   100 g
Soy, light   142 ml
Soy, dark   142 ml
Sweet and sour   200 g

Oils
Peanut
Sesame
Soy
Sunflower

Canned/bottled items
Baby sweetcorn
Bamboo shoots
Beansprouts
Dragon's eyes (loong ngaan)
Ginger, pickled
*Rice vinegar, black
Rice vinegar, red
Rice vinegar, white
Rice wine, yellow (Shaoxing)
Soya beans, black fermented   170 g
Soya beans, red fermented   170 g
Soya beans, yellow fermented   170 g
Soya beans, black paste   200 g
Soya beans, red paste   200 g
Soya beans, yellow paste   212 g

GLOSSARY

This is just a short glossary of Chinese ingredients. It lists certain items found in the text and recipes for which a further explanation is helpful. It also lists a few items which do not appear elsewhere in the book but which are used more in authentic Chinese cooking than restaurant-style cooking, and which you may encounter in specialist shops.

If an item you are seeking does not appear in the glossary then please consult the index for its reference in the text.

B

Baa Kuk Tee or We Fen – Chinese taste powder, which is a mixture of 10–12 spices and herbs. It is used like a bouquet garni as an alternative to **MSG**.

Bang Kuang – Yam (turnip-shaped) used to give texture to spring roll. Mooli can be substituted.

Bean Curd – See **Tofu**

Bokchoy – Chinese cabbage or *Pak choi*, see Chapter 9.

C

Cardamom, Green – (spice). Green pods containing aromatic black seeds. Native to China. Brought to China by traders in the centuries BC. It is an expensive spice and only used by China's Moslems.

Cassia bark – (spice). Cassia bark and cinnamon are both brown bark in pieces or quills. The inner bark of evergreen trees closely related but from different species. Both are used for the sweetness the bark imparts. Cassia is native to China, is cheaper and generally more robust. Cinnamon is native to Sri Lanka and was

taken to China and later traded to the Middle East.

Cayotte – *Fat-sau-gwa*. Pale green pears of the squash family.

Chilli Bean Sauce – Fermented black soya beans ground to a thick paste with chilli powder.

Chilli Oil – Szechwan pepper and chilli fried into oil.

Chilli Peppers – (spice). Fleshy green pods. Members of the capsicum family, which turn red when ripe. There are over 1,500 species ranging in size from tiny to large, and in heat grading from volcanic to mild. Native to Latin America and not introduced to China until the sixteenth century. They are now a part of the way of life in China's western provinces. Chinese (Schezwan) chillies are smallish and dark red and normally available dry.

Chilli Powder – Finely ground red chillies. It comes in heat gradings of normal and extra hot.

Chinese Sugar – or *Rock Sugar*. Sold in irregular sized lumps and available in various colours including white, cream, orange and brown.

183

Chinese Taste Powder – See **Baa Kuk Tee**.

Chow Chow – Pickled preserved vegetables, fruit and ginger in syrup. Canned or bottled.

Cinnamon – See **Cassia**

Citric Acid – A granular powder used by some restaurants to achieve a lemony-sour taste.

Clove – (spice). Dark brown, 'nail-shaped' (from the Latin *clavus* meaning nail). The rounded head of the clove is an unopened flower bud. Cropping is slow and expensive, and if mistimed and the flower opens, the clove is useless. Native to the Molucca Islands in Indonesia (although few grow there now), they were a major trading crop in medieval times. Today they are mainly harvested in Zanzibar, Madagascar and Grenada. One of the few spices to have remained in constant use in Britain, both in cooking (apples for example) and medicine (the oil is a soother at the dentist). They are one of the ingredients in **Chinese five-spice powder**.

Coriander – (herb). Also called *Chinese parsley*, these leaves are used widely in Chinese cookery. Coriander seeds are used only by the small Moslem community in China.

D

Doufoo – Chinese for tofu or bean curd.

Dragon's Eyes – *Loong ngaan*. Small fruit resembling the sultana, which can be substituted for it.

F

Fennel Seed – Small green seed which is very aromatic, with an aniseed taste. Used in **Chinese five-spice powder**.

Five-Spice Powder – *Ng heung fun or Wu hsiang fen*. A mixture of five aromatic spices: cinnamon, clove, fennel, star anise and Szechwan pepper. Used in Chinese cookery. Available whole or ground.

G

Garlic Chives – (herb). Flat-bladed leaf. Its leaves are larger than ordinary chives but it has, as its name states, a garlicky taste. Also called **Chinese chives**.

H

Hundred Year Eggs – or *Thousand year eggs*. These are in fact preserved in a paste of mud and lime for a few weeks. The result, when the hardened paste and shell are removed, is a dark jelly-like albumen and greeny-black yolk. It is edible but is not to the taste of most Westerners.

J

Jelly Fish, Processed – Dry shreds of jelly fish, used in stir-fries. They are unpopular in the West and are omitted from the recipes in this book.

L

Lotus Nuts – Plump, round, creamy-white shelled nuts used to give texture to dishes. Cashew nuts can be substituted.

Lotus Roots – Available fresh, canned or dried. Resembles a potato with its brown skin and white inside. When cut into discs it has attractive holes. Used as an accompaniment vegetable in stir-fries or simmered dishes.

M

Melon Shreds – Sweet pickled cucumber available from Chinese food stores.

Monosodium Glutamate (MSG) – *Vetsin* or *mei chien*. Natural crystallised extract from grains and vegetables. No taste on its own but enhances savoury flavours.

Mushroom Soy Sauce – Soy sauce flavoured with mushroom.

N

Noodle Types

DAN MEIN – Egg noodles. Round or flat, made from wheat flour. Yellow.

EE MIEN – Flat egg noodles.

FUN SIE – Cellophane or bean starch noodles. Made from moong bean starch.

HOR FUN – Thin rice noodles.

KWAY TEW – Thicker rice noodles.

MIE FUN – Very fine rice noodles or vermicelli. Good to deep-fry.

Nutmeg – (spice). Hard, round, pale brown ball. Native to South East Asia, it was introduced to the West by the earliest

Arab and Chinese traders. It is a kernel around which the lattice-like mace grows, the outer case being a pithy green fruit.

O

Orange Peel – Available dried or canned. Used as a sweetener in Western Chinese restaurants.

Oyster Sauce – Soy sauce in which oysters have been simmered. Brown and available thick or thin in bottles.

P

Pak Choi – Chinese cabbage or bokchoy. See Chaper 9.

Plum Sauce – Sauce from plums, chilli and vinegar. Used as a dip.

Potato Flour – Used as a thickener. Gives a lighter, more glazed look than cornflour.

S

Sesame Paste – Roasted white sesame seeds ground with oil. Not unlike the Middle Eastern tahine.

Sesame Oil – Extracted from roasted white sesame seeds. Dark. Wasted on heavy cooking.

Sesame Seeds – (spice). Small, flat, round, pale cream seeds. These come in other colours, including red, brown and black, the latter being used in Japanese cooking. But it is the cream seed (called white) which is used in China. It is pressed into an oil, and mixed into a paste.

Shaoxing Wine – Chinese yellow rice wine (see page 34).

Shark's Fin – Delicacy developed by Quing dynasty (1644–1911). Highly nutritional though when dry it is very hard. Use canned.

Shiu-Fu – A pickled mustard potted with herbs. Used in Szechwan cooking.

Soya Bean Curd – See **Tofu**.

Star Anise – (spice). A pretty star-shaped spice used in **Chinese five-spice powder**.

Steamed Buns – Wheat flour dough made into circular buns and steamed. Common in North China.

Szechwan Pepper – or *Flower pepper*. Reddy brown. Dried berry of a shrub. Aromatic rather than hot. One of the ingredients of **Chinese five-spice powder**.

Szechwan Vegetables – Canned mushroom cabbage or *Gai choy* in brine with chilli. Used as chutney.

T

Tofu – *Doufu*. Soft, white and cheese-like. First made during the Han dynasty (206 BC–220 AD) when an emperor required his physicians to discover new medicines. Using soy beans they came up with tofu. See page 146.

Turmeric – (spice). Fine yellow powder. Native to South Asia, turmeric is a rhizome which, like ginger, can be cooked fresh but is usually encountered ground. Used primarily for giving colour. Only used in China by the small Moslem community.

INDEX